BRIGHTER WAYS FORWARD

BRIGHTER WAYS
FORWARD

REFLECTIONS ON SPORTS, TECH, AND SOCIOECONOMIC MOBILITY

DR. MARCUS BRIGHT

DEDICATION

Mom

This book is dedicated to the life and legacy of my Mom, Mrs. Vanessa Simmons Bright. She always believed in who I was and who I could be. She gave me the incredible gift of unconditional love at the deepest level. She was deeply loved and she loved deeply. She genuinely served and cared for others.

She was the matriarch of our family – our heart, our assurance, our supporter. She was thoughtful and compassionate. She was witty and a sharp thinker. She loved watching politics and sports. She loved to cook and be with her family. She planned family reunions, made family scrapbooks, and was an archiver of family history.

She was a chief organizer of family, friends, and community. She valued education and infused the value of it in her family and all who surrounded her. She made the best of any circumstance. She would find joy in the worst situation and humor in any predicament.

She had the uncanny ability to bring a smile to people's faces and made us all laugh over and over again. She never gave up, she stayed in the race. May she continue to live through us.

Dad

I dedicate this book to my Dad, James Phillip Strong Bright. I am tremendously grateful for his sacrifice, support and consistent example of character, dependability, and compassion. He set an incredible standard for me as a man. I thank him for always being there for me and not only being an outstanding father but also playing so many other roles for me including youth sports coach, church deacon, supporter at every activity, driver on more trips to name, hospitality chair for any guest, shoulder to lean on, and values reinforcer. The way that he and my mother loved and cared for each other was an incredible sight to see and I am so blessed that God blessed me with him as my Dad.

Marcus Al

I dedicate this book to my son Marcus Al. He is a huge part of my "why" and the centerpiece of my legacy. He is extremely intelligent and has an amazing enthusiasm for life. I hope that he can gain inspiration from the words in this book and that they will help to better equip him to fulfill the purpose that God has for his life. Marcus Al is a key motivating factor behind this book and all that I do. I will always have unconditional love for him, and I thank God for the gift of his life. With God all things are possible.

Angelina

I dedicate this book to my love Angelina. She has had a transformational impact on my life in the way that she has encouraged, supported, and loved me. I am a significantly better man because of God blessing me with her in my life. Her genuine heart and ability to see mine has sparked a soul connection that I didn't even know was possible. She inspired me and to pushed me towards to completion of this book and the rediscovery of my purpose. My faith has been deepened and strengthened with her along our journey. My gratitude for her goes beyond words.

TABLE OF CONTENTS

PART I: THE ROLE OF SPORTS

PART 2: THE ROLE OF TECH

PART 3: SOCIOECONOMIC MOBILITY: EDUCATION, CAREER, AND ECONOMICS

PART 4: BRIGHTER WAYS FORWARD

PREFACE

B *righter Ways Forward: Reflections on Sports, Tech, and Socioeconomic Mobility* is a collection of essays and commentary related to sports, tech, and socioeconomic mobility in America. It will span many social issues and will contain both a multifaceted analysis of problems in each area as well as recommendations and strategies for progress and solutions.

This book will shed fresh insight into areas and issues that are especially pertinent to the upward mobility of all Americans and particularly those who come from historically marginalized communities. The content will go beneath the surface to uncover a multitude of ways to make societal advancements in key areas that have massive growth potential.

It is written in a non-linear way similar to W.E.B. DuBois "The Souls of Black Folk". The thought process behind that is with the intention of addressing a large variety of topics with there being a deeper dive into areas of focus like tech and sports.

This book is geared towards those who have an interest in being a part of meaningful social change and impact. The text will put the past and future in a context where it can be applied to the present to build bridges of access, equity, and opportunity for diverse populations of people.

There is also a sizable portion of the book that will deal with the mental, spiritual, and emotional development of individuals.

There will be an emphasis on this because communities are made up of individuals and as people become better holistic versions of themselves, communities will be uplifted in turn.

Overview

PART ONE of the book explores the multiple dimensions of how sports impact American society. I write about my personal connection to sports in multiple ways and provide a meaningful connection between my lived experiences and broader societal implications. There is a deep dive into the influence that sports have over youth, particularly Black youth. The rationale for this in-depth exploration is because there is often much more than initially meets the eye when it comes to the participation of Black youth in sports that can have dynamic ramifications for the larger community and society.

Also, Blacks are often at the bottom of many other quality of life indicators like education, employment, health, and housing. If the methods, practices, and cultural elements that have been used to produce elevated levels of performance in sports can be transferred into other areas and implemented with the same consistency then it could make the way for significant progress in the expansion of equity, access, and opportunity.

If those who are at the bottom of various quality of life indicators can be lifted, then everyone else can be elevated as well. In saying this, it is not just about a simple comparison between racial groups. It is about unlocking the dormant value and potential that is in predominantly Black communities and finding ways to create more infrastructures for people who have historically been denied an equitable shot at the American dream.

In this way, the analyzing, channeling, and expanding of the practices that have generated athletic excellence are positioned as a brighter way forward. The social and economic implications, individual and familial aspirations, and broader stakes of achieving success in the sports arena supersedes many other areas.

This may account for the tremendous overrepresentation in comparison to their percentage of the population of Blacks in the higher levels of collegiate and professional ranks in sports like basketball and football. The topic deserves an extended unpacking because of the sustained dominance and elite levels of performance in these sports despite not having superior facilities, nutrition, specialized trainers, or financial resources. In many cases, there is a deficit of these external factors when compared to other communities.

It can be deduced then that the differences lie within the individual participants and the teams that they play on. The consequences of the outsized role of sports on the lives of youth and families will be thoroughly examined and unpacked in part one. There is arguably no greater area for the potential replication and transference of infrastructures of opportunity and success than that of sports.

PART ONE begins with an examination of the role of sports and the multiple ramifications of its positioning and impact. The concept of the "athletic lottery" and the continued reliance that millions of people have in its promise and potential is thoroughly delved into. There are also lessons that are unpacked from areas of sustained athletic success as they will provide critical insight into how other pathways can be created to generate a similar level of success if they are given similar levels of support.

The term "athletic lottery" is not meant to downplay the hard work and dedication that athletes put forth perfecting his craft. It is a reference to the extremely small percentage of people who get the opportunity to play big league sports.

Some of the extensions of the athletic lottery that will be explored are college/university diversity through athletics, the pull of instant gratification, community celebration, and the mass marketing of professional athletes.

The impact of the Covid-19 pandemic and recent NCAA rule changes on the role of sports is also delved into. There may not be a group of student-athletes in the country who have been more significantly impacted by the Covid-19 pandemic than high school seniors during the Covid-19 pandemic who were aspiring to garner athletic scholarships to compete at higher educational institutions.

Athletic talent is frequently utilized as a ticket to the admission and financing of higher education for young men and women who may have not otherwise been able to access certain institutions. This increases the incentive for children and parents to place an even greater emphasis on the development of athletic talent in hopes that it will create opportunities to attend colleges and universities that can provide a higher level of academic instruction and athletic exposure.

The impact of the NCAA Name, Image, and Likeness (NIL) policy adoption on July 1, 2021 that allowed players to be able to profit from their name, image, and likeness (NIL) is explored as it has ushered in a new era for college athletics. It is an inflection point that has created a new paradigm that multiple stakeholders will have to adjust to. It represents a major deviation from a status quo that has been in place for generations as players are now able to cash in on the fame that the platform of college sports provides for the first time.

The way that the athletic identity that many student-athletes have embraced as represented by the different levels of investment in their chosen sports is also written about in part one. This investment can come in the form of effort, time, emotions, money, hopes, and dreams. Perhaps the most impactful investment that they make is the investment of their identity. This is the level of which one's view of their self is defined as being an athlete in their sport. How people define themselves and how others define them makes up their identity.

This section of part one goes further into explaining how athletes can face a crossroads when the thing that they were hanging onto, the athletic career, is gone. They can go from being celebrated to not even acknowledged after their eligibility has expired or their formal participation as player in college sports has ended. There can be a scramble to find their place in the World. A person's athletic identity investment depends on their individual valuation of the importance of being considered an athlete and how much of their identity is based on it. It varies from person to person. What is meaningful to one person may not have any meaning at all to another.

PART TWO focuses on an area that represents an avenue where the emphasis and practices that have generated success in the athletic arena can be transferred to. The example that I highlight is the role and potential of tech. Finding brighter ways forward in the area of tech is critical because there are many indicators that suggest that it will represent a sizable portion of the future of the economy. Accelerating in higher wage sectors like tech is imperative for people who are significantly less likely to be the recipients of sizable inter-generational wealth transfers and exposure to opportunity for transformational socioeconomic mobility.

They are often in the social and economic marketplace having to make it with their individual connections and income against others who are much more likely to have multiple generations of social capital and funneled down financial wealth that they can add to their own to make purchases like housing, cars, college, and investments.

The main portion of part two is a series of "Inspiring Tech" essays that focus on inspiring tech dreams, discipline, bridges, pipelines, economics, participation, on-ramps, and context. These will all represent brighter ways forward to creating an environment where people can flourish within the tech sector and enhance the quality of life of themselves and their communities through the opportunities that are connected to it.

The commentary on the role of tech highlights the importance of preparing more people to integrate into and participate in the employment and entrepreneurship opportunities that are connected to it.

PART THREE deals with socioeconomic mobility more broadly. This section is divided into three dimensions of mobility: education, career, and economics. Mobility refers to the ability to move between different levels of poverty. It entails progress in this context in the areas of economics, education, and career trajectory. The commentary and reflections in part three will cover a broad range of the ramifications of multiple factors related to all three aspects of socioeconomic mobility that will be targeted in this part.

The economic mobility section squarely addresses the economic and emotional ramifications of downward social mobility with commentary themed "broken dreams and financial illusions" that includes both an analysis of the multidimensional nature of the problem and some potential solutions. The economic ramifications of high-profile police killings is also unpacked as it is often an overlooked aspect of these unfortunate incidents.

The career mobility section goes beyond just climbing a corporate or bureaucratic ladder. It delves into deeper aspects that prevent and allow for advancement on one's chosen career pathway or pathways. This includes how perceived judgement impacts people's career choices, the factors that lead to career stagnation, how to handle career storms, career tips for college students, and how to work for a cause that is greater than one's career.

The section of educational mobility deals with issues of access, equity, and opportunity at the early childhood, secondary, and post-secondary levels of education. This includes addressing issues of race and class in higher education, enhancing counseling in K-12 schools, advocacy for high-quality after school programming, narratives around public education, college access issues, intangible factors for student success, the civil rights connection with education, course relevance for key careers, innovative college access initiatives, educational finance issues, and a case study on an exceptional student who achieved at a high level in the face of significant odds.

PART FOUR is entitled "Brighter Ways Forward" and is a combination of highlighting some policies, practices, and programs that deserve to be scaled in some way, providing insight into strategic partnerships that would likely accelerate progress in different areas. There is also a sizable portion of this part that deals with the mental, spiritual, and emotional development of individuals. There is an emphasis on this because communities are made up of individuals and as people become better holistic versions of themselves, communities will be uplifted in turn.

The internal aspects that lead to higher levels of economic and emotional viability like faith, self-esteem, internal validation, overcoming adversity, and courageously living in one's purpose is also explored in part four.

PART I: THE ROLE OF SPORTS

There is arguably no greater area for the potential replication and transference of infrastructures of opportunity and success than that of sports. We begin this journey with an examination of the role of sports and the multiple ramifications of its positioning and impact.

It was the Fall of 2007 and I had recently moved to Miami to pursue a master's degree in Public Administration. Upon arriving, I heard about a local high school, Miami Northwestern Senior High School, having the number one ranked high school football team in America according to USA Today. My brother, who was an undergraduate student at Florida International University at the time, and I decided to go to the last game that they would play in the Miami area, a state semifinals playoff game against Deerfield Beach High School.

The game was played on a Friday night in the Orange Bowl Stadium that was about three-fourths full of fans. The audience numbered in the tens of thousands. It was amazing to see this level of community support and the intensity of the game permeated throughout the crowd. This Miami Northwestern team featured seven players in their senior class who had signed to play with the University of Miami.

I had never seen such precision and excellence on a high school football field before both in the talent of the players and the sophistication of the offensive and defensive schemes that they were executing. The quarterback, Jacory Harris, ran the offense with an extremely high-level of precision along with his teammates. The fans were tremendously invested in the game and shouted both encouragement and correction at the players and coaches.

The coaches followed suit providing instruction and motivation to the players as a whole and specifically to the ones who were a part of their position groups. Each coach other than the head coach was assigned to a particular side of the football and/ or a particular position group (i.e. quarterbacks, linebackers, cornerbacks, running backs, etc.).

It was a great example of how an entire community on the macro and micro level can galvanize around a group of young men and push them to maximize and manifest their potential. Players were pushed to the edge of their ability by members of the community, parents, coaches, peers, and teammates. This standard of excellence resulted in a higher level of performance on the football field than arguably any other area in the country. They had written their own narrative for how great they could be. They did not put a limit on how many state championships they could win, how many players signed college scholarships, or how many were drafted into the NFL.

This longitudinal pipeline to success began in many cases at the age of four or five when they first began to play football. The youth football leagues in South Florida have been amongst the best breeding grounds for NFL players in the country for many years. The year-round warm weather, consistent training schedule, football culture, and constant pressure to be great all contribute to this. There is also the incalculable impact of parents, community members, and others who may be pouring their own dreams, efforts, and aspirations into the young men they strive for success and accolades on the football field.

The game sparked my reflection on broader implications and questions like what aspects lie beneath the surface and go to the root of why sports occupy such a prominent position in America. What is the impact of the positioning of sports in communities like Liberty City where Miami Northwestern Senior High School is located? How have different policies impacted the role of sports in these communities? How does the economic status of historically marginalized communities impact the positioning of sports? These are some of the questions that this book will explore.

The consistent success that has been generated in youth football in Miami and South Florida has persisted in the face of significant economic odds. The area has been plagued by extreme economic inequality, increasingly unaffordable housing, and opportunity gaps in other areas like education and healthcare.

The demographics of Miami-Dade County, for example, are drastically different from any other county in the United States. Nearly 58% of the county's population was born outside of the United States. This is more than ten percent higher than the second closest metropolitan area, Santa Ana, CA.

A study from the Corporation for Enterprise Development (CFED) entitled "The Racial Wealth Divide in Miami" revealed that Black people in Miami make $14,388 less and have a 1.6 percent higher unemployment rate (15%) than Blacks nationally. The Hispanic population makes $13,910 less than their counterparts nationally and has an 8% unemployment rate (Corporation for Enterprise Development, 2016).

The report noted that "each Latino ethnic group enjoys better economic outcomes overall than do the city's black residents. Haitians and African-Americans are more likely than other major ethnic groups to live in poverty with poverty rates of 45% and 44% respectively." Additionally, the middle white household makes three times the annual income of the middle household of color. White makes $70,575 on average while Latinos and Blacks make $28,486 and $21,212 respectively (Corporation for Enterprise Development, 2016).

Overall, Miamians pay a higher percentage of their income on housing than anywhere else in the country. This causes an increasingly high number of people to go into a survival mode where it is a fight to make ends meet. This is a predicament that hard work and education alone will not solve. Miami's deeply segregated neighborhoods date back many decades to legally enforced segregation and discriminatory housing policy. The overtly discriminatory public policy of the past has given way to the more subtle and coded barriers of the present.

Black children lag behind in almost every other area outside of athletics. This alone warrants a deep dive into what practices and processes are in place that have produced a prolonged period of elevated performance across time and location. This is not to say that every predominately Black sports team is successful. There are predominately Black athletic teams and programs that have losing records on an annual basis and predominately White teams who win championships year after year. This phenomenon is not based on an absolute truth or even completely raced based. The desire to be great in sports and aspire to compete at the highest level transcends race, class, and geography.

It is the case though that athletics is often one of the only beacons of excellence in communities that are dominated by substandard schools, high dropout rates, dilapidated housing, abject poverty, illegal drugs, unemployment, violence, and despair.

I am a former basketball player who went to college on a basketball scholarship. This book is not meant to be anti-athlete or to discourage participation in athletics. It's hard to fault kids for wanting to pursue their dreams. I had my own hoop dreams growing up. Sports plays and has played an outsized role in my own life. I grew up playing basketball, soccer, and baseball. My Mom stopped me from playing football despite my adamant objection. I ended up playing basketball in college and have been a sports fan for years.

I'm originally from a town in Tennessee by the name of Martin. It is located in the northwest corner of the state about 10 miles from the Kentucky border. It is a college town that contains the University of Tennessee at Martin. Many of the people that I grew up with came to Martin through the university in some form including both of my parents who met while being affiliated with the school.

My biggest influences were my parents. They served as a tremendous source of consistency, stability, and support. I am grateful for the values that they instilled in me. They taught me through their words and actions the importance of service, unselfishness, responsibility, compassion, and loyalty.

I am a member of the first generation of my family on my mother's side not to pick cotton. My mom, Vanessa Simmons Bright, grew up one of five children in the rural West Tennessee town of Alamo. Her parents, Burnell Simmons Sr. and Lula Mae Cole Simmons, grew up in an earlier period of time where a large number of Black families were sharecroppers or tenant farmers.

My Mom and her siblings grew up picking cotton, but not under the sharecropping arrangement like their parents did. Nevertheless, it is a humble reminder for me of what it is that the generations that came before me endured and the limited scope of opportunities that they had in comparison to what I have.

Every February, my Mom would decorate the halls of our home church, Fuller Street Missionary Baptist Church in Dresden, TN, for Black History Month. She would put up pictures of people who made a significant impact on the movement for the progress of Black people in America. Some were more famous than others. All made their own meaningful contribution to some area of society. There would be posters and displays that showed the picture of people like Frederick Douglass, Harriet Tubman, Phyllis Wheatley, Dr. Charles Drew, W.E.B. DuBois, Malcolm X, and Dr. Martin Luther King Jr. along with a description of their life.

I believe that the value that my parents placed on their contributions took root in me and gave me an appreciation for them as well. I began to become very much aware of the sacrifices and great feats that preceded my arrival in this World and wanted to make a similar impact during my allotted time. Without even consciously knowing this, this has seeped into my consciousness and had become a part of my DNA. It had become a part of my purpose and the destiny that I believe that I must fulfill.

I began playing basketball at a very young age. My Dad was the initial driver of my passion for playing the game. He had come to Martin in the early 1970s on a basketball scholarship to the University of Tennessee at Martin. His 6'4 frame and exploits on the court at Fayetteville Central High School in the middle Tennessee town of Fayetteville had brought him to west Tennessee.

I could sense his interest in the game and that probably drove me to want to play it even more. Basketball served as so many different things growing up. It was an escape that would occupy most of my free time until I left Martin at the age of 18. It showed me the importance of practice and persistence. I took to it naturally as a game that you could practice for hours by yourself and then go see the results of that practice manifest itself in competition.

It was also something that was celebrated and elevated in a way that nothing else was as it pertain to youth in the area. The value that society and the people in my town had put on sports served as an extra piece of external motivation to drive my basketball aspirations. I knew from an early age that the game of basketball could take me different places and create different opportunities for me moving forward. I saw it as my ticket out of Martin, to college, and maybe even a career in the professional ranks.

I learned how to play with other people, how to overcome adversity, how to be persistent, and how to self-assess and identify weaknesses in my own game that I needed to improve. This all translates to other areas of life. The mental and physical preparation and execution that is needed to achieve success in basketball is something that can be used to develop a formula for success across the board. The problem is that too many people don't recognize the transferability of those traits, habits, and abilities that they cultivated playing sports and how they

8

can bring value for years to come after one's formal years of playing competitive athletics have passed.

My reason for being in Miami goes beyond the year-round warm weather and panoramic beaches. My heart was drawn to the diverse communities of South Florida from the time that I arrived at 18 years old. I have long felt that the core of the some of my most valuable contributions would be left in its communities.

This conviction was intensified when I worked as a Student-Athlete Academic Coordinator at Florida International University. I had the opportunity to work daily with student-athletes from numerous sports teams to help foster their academic and social development. As I got to know them, I got to know more and more about the schools and communities where they had come from. They had come from high schools like Miami Northwestern in Liberty City, Booker T. Washington in Overtown, Miami Carol City in Miami Gardens, and other similar communities in Florida.

My mind and efforts went to not only assisting them but also to what could be done from a collective standpoint to create infrastructures of opportunity for the thousands of other students who did not come to college via athletic scholarships. In a way they were amongst the winners of the athletic lottery. This is not to diminish their hard work in athletics to land them the scholarships, but to acknowledge the very limited number of college sports scholarships then compared to the number of people who play high school sports. I wondered what the thousands of other children were doing after they finished high school.

The Athletic Lottery

The "athletic lottery" and the continued reliance that millions of people have in its promise and potential is a topic worth delving into. There are also lessons that can be learned from areas of sustained athletic success as it can provide critical insight into how other pathways can be created to generate a similar level of success if they are given similar levels of support.

The term "athletic lottery" is not meant to downplay the hard work and dedication that athletes put forth perfecting their craft. It is a reference to the extremely small percentage of people who get the opportunity to play big league sports. According to data from the National Collegiate Athletic Association (NCAA) website, out of 540,000 high school basketball participants 3.5% go on to play in the NCAA with 1.0% going to Division I schools, 1.0% to Division II schools, and 1.4% to Division III schools. Out of 18,816 participants in men's basketball and 4,181 draft eligible athletes 1.2% (52) compete in major professional athletics. Out of 1,006,013 high school football participants 7.3% go on to play in the NCAA with 2.9% going to Division I schools, 1.9% to Division II schools, and 2.5% to Division III schools. Out of 73,712 participants in football and 16,380 draft eligible athletes 1.6% (254) compete in major professional athletics (National Collegiate Athletic Association, n.d.).

The traditional lottery where large amounts of money is awarded to a few lucky people does not have the same level of overreliance that the athletic lottery has. People in large part do not solely focus on winning that lottery. Those that play surely daydream about what it would be like to win, but they do not abandon other routes to success in the way that far too many young people do in their pursuit of careers in professional basketball and football.

There has been a great deal of discussion and consternation about the status of Black males in America specifically and people of color more broadly. One of the greatest infrastructures of opportunity for young Black males has been athletics. There are many positive aspects to playing sports including the development of discipline, teamwork, and conditioning in addition to providing an alternative to potentially destructive idle time. Sporting events serve as a gathering place and a source of community pride for families and communities.

Sports has long been a fixture in American life generally and in Black communities more specifically. It has served and serves different roles for different people. Sports is everything from a way to get exercise to a community gathering point to a way to make a living to a vehicle of social mobility to an avenue to develop teamwork and social skills in people.

It has been used to break down barriers like Jackie Robinson in Major League Baseball, foster diplomacy on international stage like Jesse Owens in the 1936 Olympics, and fight for social causes like Muhammed Ali in the 1960 and 1970s. The role of sports in America is broad and wide ranging. This book will examine sports from the lens of an aspirational tool and vehicle for social mobility.

While sports may play the role of a hobby to some individuals, others may see it as their sole means of social mobility. Sports, particularly football and basketball, occupy an extremely prominent aspirational place in the minds of many. The reasons for this are manifold. There is of course the pure enjoyment and the love of playing sports. They receive consistent support and validation from their peers and community. They are cheered for and celebrated for their talent.

The athletic lottery has been created by a combination of social and economic incentives. According to the American Psychological Association "socioeconomic status is the social standing or class of an individual group. It is often measured as a combination of education, income, and occupation. Examinations of socioeconomic status often reveal inequities in access to resources, plus issues related to privilege, power, and control" (American Psychological Association, n.d.).

There are social incentives that motivate people to go excel in sports like the applause and celebration that they receive from a community's high valuation on winning sports performance and an elevated status among their peers. The motivation of young people who pursue sports varies. Some have bought into the narrative that a particular sport is the "ticket out". Some enjoy the social experience of playing a sport with their friends and being a part of a team. There are those who have parent(s) who place a major emphasis on sports and want to receive approval and affirmation from them in the space. This sentiment can go further through a desire to fulfill the sports expectation and/or aspiration of other member(s) of their family who may want to vicariously fulfill their sports dream through their young relative who is currently engaged in the sport.

The motivation of a college or professional athlete may be more explicitly connected to an economic benefit that is attached to participation. Sports can afford some student-athletes with admission and financial aid coverage at a college or university that they may not have otherwise been able to attend. Participation in sports can also give one access to significant financial wealth or at least create the aspiration of using sports as a vehicle to attain it. This incorporates more of a transactional relationship where a scholarship or contract is exchanged for "labor" in the form one's participation in a sport. There are also those who support their financial livelihood by working as a coach, administrator, or in some other sports-related occupation.

Throughout the history of America, the government has played a major role in limiting or cutting off major avenues of social mobility and economic opportunity. An environment of economic deprivation and desperation is one of the biggest feeders of the athletic lottery.

The late rapper The Notorious B.I.G. referred to a perception of the options for urban males in the song "Things Done Changed" by saying that "the streets is a short shop. Either you're slingin' crack rock, or you got a wicked jump shot." He was articulating a part of the sense of economic desperation that many people feel when their options for financial prosperity seem to be extremely limited. When "conventional" routes seem to be closed off, a narrow focus on the routes that appear to be more open like athletics can be heightened.

When economic conditions are extreme, one can feel more inclined to go to more extreme measures to survive and prosper. One of these extreme measures can be an elevated level of athletic performance with the hopes that it will be a vehicle to elevate their financial status. The concept of economic desperation is not one that is based only on anecdotal stories. There is a mountain of wealth data that paints a clear picture of the economic state of Black America.

The data is conclusive that the economic conditions of Black people in America are extreme when compared to other groups. A report entitled *The economic state of Black America: What is and what could be* "estimated "a $300 billion disparity between Black and white families in the annual flow of new wealth, some 60 percent of which comes from intergenerational transfers. Every year there is a massive intergenerational transfer of family wealth, creating an effect that is both profound and self-perpetuating. Black families are less likely to receive inheritances, and when they do, the amounts are smaller. The gap in inheritances between Black and white recipients is some $200 billion annually" (Stewart, Chui, et al., 2021).

In addition, the Harvard Business Review estimates that there is "a $220 billion annual wage disparity with Black workers concentrated in lower-wage jobs, underrepresented in higher-paying occupations, and paid less, on average, than white workers in the same occupational categories, especially in managerial and leadership roles" (Stewart, Pinder, & Chui, 2021).

The fragility of the low wage market leaves people living with a sense of desperation. This often entails long stints of unemployment, underemployment, and employment discrimination. This may entice people to go into the underground economy to meet basic needs. There is also a portion of students who come from low socioeconomic backgrounds who grow up with a feeling of inadequacy that can last throughout adulthood. Economic deprivation has the capacity to crush the self-esteem of students, parents, and communities.

An argument can be made that there is simply more at stake on average for Black athletes because of the economic conditions of Black people in the United States. The stakes are raised and there can be the impression that more is one the line. This enhances the allure of the "athletic lottery" as a "way out" and many young people see sports as their best route to a college scholarship.

As a reminder, the term "athletic lottery" is a reference to the small percentage of athletes who receive college athletic scholarships or professional contracts versus the very large number of people who are vying for them. This usage of the term in this piece is not intended to diminish the dedication and hard work that athletes put toward honing their skills and talent.

Athletic talent is utilized at young ages as a ticket to private schools that are located both in their home city and in other parts of the country. This increases the incentive for children and parents to place an even greater emphasis on the development of athletic talent based on the possibility that it will create opportunities to attend better resourced schools that can provide a higher level of academic instruction and athletic exposure.

Symbols of athletic transcendence also play a key role in providing examples of how winning the athletic lottery can provide economic deliverance from a prior condition of economic desperation. This plays out in cities all over the country where certain players inspire a generation of younger players to follow their journey. The symbolic power of these examples is even more potent when a native of their neighborhood makes it into the professional ranks. This is the ever-present dream that dominates the mind of urban athletes. Examples of players who had this kind of impact on their home areas are Isiah Thomas in Chicago, Anfernee "Penny" Hardaway in Memphis, and Dwayne "Pearl" Washington in

New York City.

These examples of athletic lottery winners create narratives that people can identify with and apply to their own lives. Widespread buy in eventually leads to a greater level of embeddedness and adoption for large populations of people. This greatly influences how both individuals and broader communities think and behave. Elements that create mass participation in the athletic lottery eventually become a taken for granted aspect of life that is considered common and "par for the course."

The growth and proliferation of the athletic lottery is based on many people buying into the belief that they too can win despite there being significant odds against it. Many young people have the illusion of there being a much greater likelihood that they will reach the professional ranks than they actually have. The odds of getting there are slim to none regardless of one's desire to get there.

The few athletes who emerge and gain access to the upper levels of college and professional athletics are treated much differently from the majority of Black people in the United States. Black males, in particular, receive a celebration and adoration in the athletic arena that they find in no other area of society. The economic desperation that is prevalent in a large number of communities creates a sense of urgency in many student-athletes where they feel that their lives will be cut short or will be lackluster if they don't escape the environment where they were raised.

The economic status of Black America is one of the multi-faceted elements of the athletic lottery that contains more than what may initially meet the eye or be at the forefront of one's mind. It is important to unpack the placement and potency of athletics in predominately Black communities and explore the various dimensions of this phenomenon. The more we can study this area that has consistently produced greatness against considerable odds, the more we can potentially institutionalize this excellence into other areas.

The example of former Dallas Cowboys wide receiver Dez Bryant is a good illustration of what the athletic lottery is about. Bryant made headlines in 2017 with his comments on Instagram about the issue of race. Bryant expressed his support for the following remarks from NBA Hall of Famer Charles Barkley: "We as Black people we're never going to be successful not because you white people but because of other Black people." Bryant stated that "I hate to admit it but I understand the quote" (Fisher, 2017).

Bryant wrote in an additional passage that "instead of making videos about the history of racism that get applause or people with influence merely doing things to post for social media we should focus on individual accountability as a whole" (Fisher, 2017). Bryant was not wrong in my opinion in his call for individual accountability, but he was wrong in his failure to acknowledge the formidable forces that systematically black opportunities from many Black people. His refusal to acknowledge the significant amount of deeply entrenched barriers that people face suggests that he may have fallen into an athletic version of "The Sunken Place" (Bright, 2017b).

The Sunken Place is a reference to the movie "Get Out" where Black people are hypnotized into disconnecting themselves from the plight of the broader Black population. Bryant acts as if his journey to NFL stardom is a replicable path for the masses of Black men. He seems unaware that he hit the athletic lottery.

As a result of winning the athletic lottery, Bryant is treated much differently from the majority of Black men in the United States. Black males receive a celebration and adoration in the athletic arena that they find in no other area of society. Meanwhile, the vast sum of Black males who throw their everything into sports, but whose talent did not warrant college athletic scholarship offers or pro sports contracts are often those with the least access to viable post-secondary and employment options. As hip-hop artist Jay Z once stated; "I've seen hoop dreams deflate like a true fiend's weight." The parading of those fortunate few that win the athletic lottery masks the struggles of the Black community at large (Bright, 2017b).

Bryant also referenced a friend of his who spent his adulthood dealing drugs and wished he had chosen a different path. There is certainly no excuse for engaging in the drug trade, but the lack of gainful employment options that many Blacks face can also not be discounted. A study from the U.S. Census Bureau's American Community Survey found that several cities including Chicago, Washington, D.C., Philadelphia, and Baltimore with jobless rates of over 45% for non-institutionalized Black men between the ages of 20 and 34. In several urban areas there is a jobless rate of 40% to 50% for Black men (Cherry, 2016). This prompts some of Bryant's non-professional athlete peers to develop behaviors that go against mainstream norms in a quest to reach their economic aspirations.

Bryant himself told Sports Day in 2010 that "the reason my Mom sold drugs and went to jail is so we could live…She paid a hard price for it. Now she doesn't even have to do anything like that again. God put me in a position to help my family and others who have helped me" (Taylor, 2015). Surely, Bryant must see all of those people who look like him that God didn't put in a position to play in the NFL. If not for being a recipient in the athletic lottery, Bryant may very well have found himself unable to find employment after being arrested on domestic violence charges in 2012.

Most Black men who have faced such charges have an additional level of difficulty finding employment. There is often no margin for error in a criminal justice system that feeds off of the mistakes or alleged missteps of Black men. Dez Bryant's intentions with his comments were likely good, but he needs to acknowledge that there is a mass incarceration and economic crisis in Black America that scoring touchdowns can't solve.

The Pull of Instant Gratification

Byum et al. (2009) contended that the tendency for young people to engage in activities that fulfill immediate gratification could result in civic disengagement or a reduction in time devoted to schoolwork. An explanation for this according to Byum may lie in a chronic inability to engage in experiences that entail a payoff that is delayed as opposed to a reflection of values that are misguided. An environment where options that are immediately gratifying are readily available encourages the inability significantly (Byun et al. 2009). Bembenutty and Karabenick (2004) posited that the success of students depends in a significant way on the ability to resist immediately gratifying temptations in favor of a more substantial long-term goal.

Adler and Adler (1991) described the conflict between instant and delayed gratification that exists in the lives of athletes: "Athletes also faced a conflict between their pulls toward immediate versus long-term reinforcement. Athletic participation gave them immediate positive feedback for their efforts in the forms of adoring fans, media attention, praise and rewards from the coaching staff, and the admiration of their peers. These were very intense forms of gratification. Academic participation, in contrast, was something that would not pay off for them until some time in the future. Before they could reap any benefits they had to finish four years of college and graduate. Even then, their reward would be a job (hopefully) and a secure lifestyle. This was hardly a challenge to the allure of a possible professional basketball career, despite the slim odds of their making it. Most athletes came from backgrounds that favored the immediate, rather than deferred, forms of gratification. Yet even those who came from middle class families soon succumbed to the orientation toward the immediate, and succumbed to the ethos of 'cashing in' on the rewards for all their hard work in the present time" (Adler & Adler, p. 150).

Adler and Adler (1991) suggest that this pull of instant gratification prompted them to put everything they had into the present at the expense of their long-term future. In many instances, long-term planning outside of athletics is non-existent.

Their athletic identity is often created and nurtured at the detriment to other aspect of their development. With all of their attention on athletics; the students did not put in enough time to develop the study habits, knowledge, and skills to compete in the academic arena. Their inability to compete on a high academic level led to feelings of alienation and nihilism towards scholastic endeavors.

Coaches often don't have to spend much time encouraging their players to focus on their sports; athletes generally encourage themselves to concentrate on their primary common interest. They often build upon existing norms and values that are already established in their peer culture. The athletes collectively go through an intensive process that socializes them to the experiences of the athletic arena. Majority rule is often the norm in these groups and they establish demands and rewards on these premises. Generally, they treat their sport as their career and do everything they can to maximize their chances of success (Adler & Adler, 1991; Brooks, 2009).

Community Celebration

Neighborhood and community celebration of sports is a major factor in the consistent production of athletic excellence. Many communities enthusiastically value sports and respect superior performance. This setting bolsters the view of sports as a career, dream, and identity (Brooks, 2009). Older members of the community will mentor young athletes in their sport because the community if often invested in their success. When the neighborhood high school sports team is successful; the whole community feels pride and the gaining of bragging rights over other rival communities.

Community adulation is even more prevalent when a native of their neighborhood makes it into the professional ranks. This is the ever-present dream that dominates the mind of many athletes. Aside from the sheer joy of playing their particular sports, youth often get great satisfaction and a feeling of superiority at being able to master something that gives them glory. They were also often encouraged by their peers, parents, and community to maximize their athletic ability (Messner,

1989). There are few other places for most people where they will see their community openly cheering for them outside of sports.

The thousands of people who fill stadiums for games represent approval and value. Approval and value are two things that many young men yearn for. They seek approval and they want to be valued. When thousands show up for sporting events and only a handful show up for other events that focus on academics then that consciously or unconsciously signals that what they are watching is of tremendous importance.

There is strength in numbers and the game reason why activists seek to gather large numbers for a protest, or a rally is the same reason why the impact of the packed gyms are stadiums for games are potent. They both signal importance and value. This is part of the cultural embeddedness of how society has placed additional value on certain sports and certain sporting events. This additional value makes all the difference.

The lottery is based on many people buying into the belief that they too can win against significant odds. Even when it defies financial sense, they can be the one that does make it. Making it would mean in a level of extreme value and approval being ascribed to them. This is a part of the intangible allure of the athletic lottery. Part of what is taken for granted is that what is considered common and "par for the course" is rarely questioned or examined.

Mass Marketing of Professional Athletes

The lifestyle of the professional athlete that is mass marketed and promoted to the broader public is easily transferrable to lifestyles that are promoted by hip hop artists. Hip hop music is consumed by millions of young people daily for a significant amount of time. The music and the messages seep into the subconscious. There are many positive messages of drive and determination, but there are also a countless number of songs and music videos that advertise and promote a lifestyle of beautiful women, big houses, fancy cars, and carefree living.

It can paint the picture of heaven on earth, especially to young and impressionable minds. The over-the-top, braggadocious rap rhyme of many artists are congruent with the lifestyle picture that is painted by athletes on social media and other platforms. The images and narratives feed the psyche and hunger of communities and individuals alike. It is almost like a fantasy world that becomes even more in reach when individuals from one's community achieves athletic lottery status.

What is the difference between a game with talented athletes that is played in an empty gym that no spectators see and a game that is televised and promoted to viewers all over the world? Marketing. Mass marketing is an extremely powerful tool. Marketing that is backed by significant capital resources can make what is obscure mainstream and people that are unknown instantly famous. What is made visible and important to the masses can be carefully cultivated and displayed with the goal of having a certain effect.

Capital and the media at large can decide to direct attention, support, and promotion to whatever people and behaviors that they choose. Communities and individuals that are organized can do the same. It begins with a set of definitive decisions until it becomes institutionalized after a period.

Salaries of professional athletes are consistently promoted and mass marketed. The salaries of coaches at the NCAA Division I universities and professional leagues are very substantial. These financial incentives are motivation to keep young men in the athletic pipeline. A prized recruit that is under the tutelage of a certain coach can be a vehicle for that coach to follow the player an elevated level of the sport via a position on a coaching or operations staff.

The Impact of the Covid-19 Pandemic and NCAA Rule Changes on Sports and the Role of Sports

There may not be a group of student-athletes in the country who have been more significantly impacted by the Covid-19 pandemic than high school seniors during the Covid-19 pandemic who were aspiring to garner athletic scholarships to compete at higher educational institutions.

Athletic talent is frequently utilized as a ticket to the admission and financing of higher education for young men and women who may have not otherwise been able to access certain institutions. This increases the incentive for children and parents to place an even greater emphasis on the development of athletic talent in hopes that it will create opportunities to attend colleges and universities that can provide a higher level of academic instruction and athletic exposure.

The cultural embeddedness of the athletic route and the sports dream in the lives of young Black men in particular is something that is taken for granted in most cases. While sports may play the role of a hobby to some individuals, others see it as the sole means to social mobility. Sports, particularly football and basketball occupy an extremely prominent aspirational place in the minds of many young Black males. The reasons for this are manifold. There is of course the pure enjoyment and the love of playing sports. They also receive consistent support and validation from their peers and community. They are cheered for and celebrated for their talent.

Those few athletes who emerge and gain access to the upper levels of college and professional athletics are treated much differently from the majority of Black men in the United States. Black males receive a celebration and adoration in the athletic arena that they find in no other area of society.

Unfortunately, the vast sum of Black males who throw their everything into sports, but whose talent did not warrant college athletic scholarship offers or pro sports contracts are often those with the least access to viable post-secondary education and employment options. Those young people who fall into that category may be the most impacted by decisions to cancel entire sports seasons.

A case study for the impact of the Covid-19 pandemic on youth sports and the aspiration attached to it is the Shelby County Schools (TN) System decision to cancel Fall and Winter Sports during the 2020-2021 school year. Shelby County, which encompasses the city of Memphis, is the largest school district with the greatest number of minority student-athletes in the state of Tennessee. Memphis has long been a hotbed for basketball talent and has increasingly produced a significant number of blue-chip football recruits.

Shelby County Schools was the only school district in the state to take the stance of having no sports participation at all. The announcement from Shelby County Schools Superintendent Dr. Joris Ray on September 15, 2020 read as follows – "Today, the District announced that fall sports are postponed until further notice. Despite collaborative efforts in the District and locally to reduce the spread of the Coronavirus, there is still far too much uncertainty to move forward with athletic practices and competitions at this time. SCS leaders have been working closely with the CDC, Health Department, and National Federation of State High School Associations (NFHS), and all of them have warned about the risks of spreading the virus through athletic participation at this time. Local infectious disease specialist Dr. Manoj Jain also recently cautioned that sports are not a wise idea 'given the uncertainties around the novel virus and the undiagnosed number of cases in our community.' Our decision to postpone fall sports until further notice is yet another unimaginable consequence of an unprecedented time. However, we must lean on the guidance of health experts and not emotions (Sweeney, 2020). We want to play, our coaches want to coach, and we still hope for the opportunity to do both when conditions improve."

The largest population of Black boys in the state who had some level of attachment and dependence on pursuing the athletic route to a college scholarship found themselves completely shut out of sports at their schools as a result of this decision.

The District's decision was met with tremendous opposition from a segment of coaches, players, parents, and a large part of the broader community. The opposition was driven by a sense of unfairness, given that the rest of the state was playing including all of the bordering county schools and special school districts within Shelby County such as Arlington, Collierville, and Bartlett.

Another issue driving the opposition was the plight of so many players who were depending on their senior seasons to showcase their ability to college coaches with the hopes of garnering athletic scholarships. There was additional anguish in the community about a perceived lack of compromise from the district. They did not even attempt to play one game.

Some felt misled by the initial declaration of the season being postponed and not cancelled. This left many student-athletes dangling with false hope when they could have made a more informed decision if they would have known earlier that the entire season would not take place.

The Superintendent, who also happened to be a Black male, pointed out that he was following the guidance of health experts and not emotions. The predominately Black population of Memphis over-indexes in pre-existing health conditions like diabetes, hypertension, and high blood pressure that are particularly susceptible to Covid-19.

One example of the impact of this Shelby County Schools ruling was a Senior student-athlete from a Memphis high school football powerhouse who had been anticipating his senior season on the field. He had previously played more of a reserve role on a senior-laden team the season before. Though he had the stature and athleticism of a Division I football player, he did not yet have an adequate amount of game film to fully display his talent in the eyes of many college recruiters.

He and his teammates were anticipating that they would be getting an opportunity to play at some point when the initial postponement announcement was made. Many of them had been working toward this season since they first began playing the sport several years prior. At first, they had all been attending practice every day with the hopes of having the opportunity to display their talent in front of college coaches or at least getting some quality game film that they could send to coaching staffs. As time went on and the prospects for having a season began to dwindle, so did attendance at practice. Coaches were challenged with sustaining morale and pushing the student-athletes to continue to hone their craft even with no promise of an opportunity to display their talent on the horizon.

Players responded in a number of different ways. Some transferred to other schools that were located in districts where competition was taking place. Others stopped coming to practice and picked up jobs. Another group of those who stopped coming to practice found themselves engaged with gangs and other nefarious endeavors. The combination of not being required to physically be in school or football practice left an abundance of discretionary time that had the potential ending up being dangerous and/or unproductive if not appropriately channeled.

There was another group who continued going to practice and held out hope for combines or other showcase events to potentially be seen by recruiters. Fortunately for this senior, he was reared in a household that prioritized and required academic excellence from the very beginning. He maintained a stellar grade point average and the cancelled season gave him additional time to prepare for the ACT and SAT tests. He had hopes of getting an athletic scholarship, but he was not dependent on it.

He had more of a well-rounded view and repertoire of guidance and experiences that offered multiple avenues to get to his desired destination. He is positioned to attend an institution of higher education via academic scholarship and then still play sports at the collegiate level as a "walk on" if he chooses. This actually gives him a lot more agency over his own future than going on an athletic scholarship where his scholarship could be based on the frequently shifting coaching dynamics of his team.

This autonomy will serve him well at the next level because he will be more likely than other student-athletes to go into a major of his true choice and not one directed by student-athletic academic counselors who may be more interested in keeping him eligible than putting him in a position that will lead to gainful employment and an expanded set of economic opportunities.

There are lessons to be learned from what took place in Shelby County Schools sports during the Fall of 2020. The school district could have been clearer about their long-term plans to cancel the season. The ambiguity may have stemmed from the fear of a mass exodus of students leaving to pursue athletic participation in other districts where competition was being allowed. The decision and course of action from Shelby County Schools may have indeed all been about guidance from health experts, but their roll out and distribution of information has caused some to raise their eyebrows.

Many in the Memphis youth sports community that includes players, parents, coaches, and supporters received a harsh wake-up call about the downside of an overreliance on the athletic lottery. The previously unthinkable cancellation of a season has no doubt altered the perception and placement of sports for some. Hopefully, other routes of development and exposure were opened to young people in the absence of competitive sports, and this perceived setback for Memphis area athletes will eventually be a setup for a more holistic view of who these young people are and who they can become.

NCAA Name, Image, and Likeness (NIL)

The NCAA adoption of a new policy on July 1, 2021 that allowed players to be able to profit from their name, image, and likeness (NIL) has ushered in a new era for college athletics. It is an inflection point that will create a new paradigm that multiple stakeholders will have to adjust to. It represents a major deviation from a status quo that has been in place for generations. Players will now be able to cash in on the fame that the platform of college sports provides for the first time (Hosick, 2021).

It is a monumental victory for the economic empowerment of student-athletes that removes the shackles that previously restricted players from being able to profit from their name, image, and likeness. It opens the possibility for life changing financial resources to go to families who may have been historically excluded from other wealth building opportunities. The overwhelming majority of student-athletes will not make it to the NBA, NFL, or other professional leagues. Their window to economically benefit from their athletic prowess expires when their college eligibility does. This one reason why NIL ruling is incredibly important.

The quick passage of this measure with little regulation and relatively vague instructions has left a lot of open room for how it will ultimately be implemented. The NCAA issued the following guidance (Hosick, 2021):

- "Individuals can engage in NIL activities that are consistent with the law of the state where the school is located. Colleges and universities may be a resource for state law questions.

- College athletes who attend a school in a state without an

NIL law can engage in this type of activity without violating NCAA rules related to name, image and likeness.

- Individuals can use a professional services provider for NIL activities.

- Student-athletes should report NIL activities consistent with state law or school and conference requirements to their school."

The NCAA made a distinction between NIL and schools directly paying players by stating that "while opening name, image and likeness opportunities to student-athletes, the policy in all three divisions preserves the commitment to avoid pay-for-play and improper inducements tied to choosing to attend a particular school. Those rules remain in effect" (Hosick, 2021, para. 5)

Though it is not a formal pay for play situation, the opportunities for student-athletes and their families to financially benefit from this ruling are substantial. The term that I have previously used to describe the pursuit of sports stardom, "the athletic lottery", has become even more relevant with this ruling and preceding declarations from the NCAA over the past year (Bright, 2021b). There are many more eligible student-athletes competing for the same number of spots on college sports rosters with players being granted an additional year of eligibility (Hosick, 2020a) and the one-time transfer rule being put in place (Hosick, 2020b). These spots also have much more lucrative potential now with the passage of the new NIL ruling.

This rule change from the NCAA comes on the heels of the Supreme Court ruling in the NCAA v. Alston case on June 21, 2021 that involved a group of current and former student-athletes "challenging the NCAA's restrictions on compensation.

Specifically, they alleged the NCAA's rules violate the Sherman Act, which prohibits 'contract(s), combination(s), or conspiracy(ies) in restraint of trade or commerce" according to the court's ruling. Justice Brett Kavanaugh gave a blistering critique of the NCAA that could open up the floodgates for future lawsuits. Kavanaugh wrote that sports traditions "cannot justify the NCAA's decision to build a massive money-raising enterprise on the backs of student-athletes who are not fairly compensated. Nowhere else in America can business get away with agreeing not to pay their workers a fair market rate…. The NCAA is not above the law" (National Collegiate Athletic Association Vs. Alston, 21/06/2021).

The momentum that was manufactured by college basketball players before the NCAA Tournament using the hashtag #NotNCAAProperty (Wamsley, 2021) and a set of NIL state policies that became effective on July 1 in Alabama, Florida, Georgia, Mississippi, New Mexico, and Texas also played pivotal roles in pushing the NCAA to make this new ruling (Sallee, 2021).

While this policy change on NIL offers some new possibilities of benefits to accrue to student-athletes, it should be acknowledged that players have been able to benefit from their participation in college athletics in other ways. Many student-athletes have been afforded admission and financial aid coverage at a college or university that they would not otherwise have been able to attend. There are also those who have been able to utilize connections that they gained from participation in athletics to open doors of opportunity in other areas of life.

This new measure is not a one size fits all dynamic. There will be costs and casualties to go along with the benefits and opportunities. The right thing to do is not always the easiest thing to do. The implementation of NIL may be unregulated, uneven, and unequal. There will be a backlash and there will be drawbacks. Donors who may have contributed to athletic departments may opt to provide endorsement deals directly to student-athletes. This may cause a reduction in the number of overall sports that are offered by college and university athletic departments. There will likely be a redistribution of resources and revenues in several areas related to college athletics.

There are many athletic departments and sports programs that operate in the red. They cost more money than they bring in. The major programs that bring in massive amounts of money could be categorized as outliers. The rank-and-file college athletics program does not generate enough revenue to sustain itself and is funded by student fees and other budget allocations from the college or university's general funding sources (National Collegiate Athletic Association, 2015).

Other challenges that may come are additional distractions for student-athletes, increased jealousy among players who sign varying levels of endorsement deals, fractures in team cohesion, and recruiting based purely on NIL opportunities. Questions abound about how the prospect recruiting process will change, what role AAU teams and coaches will play, and who will ultimately be permitted to "represent" players in terms of helping them to secure NIL opportunities.

These are all questions that will be answered over time, but in the meantime a relatively unregulated NIL environment will proceed. Nonetheless, as with other seismic changes that have happened, people and institutions will adjust. It is a new world of possibilities with those who have positioned themselves to be able to seize this window of opportunity most likely to be the initial beneficiaries.

This disruption in the economic arrangement and distribution in NCAA athletics is long overdue. The system of everyone getting a big piece of the financial pie except for the players who people pay to see play was and is unjust. A new paradigm is here for college athletics and a more equitable share of revenue and resources is on the way.

New Transfer Rules

ESPN commentator Dick Vitale described the NCAA transfer portal as "out of control" in an April 9, 2021 tweet referring to the over 1,200 players who were in the portal looking for new programs to play for. The system of NCAA athletics is undergoing a new shake up where control seems to be up for grabs. The COVID-19 pandemic has given many players an extra year of eligibility (Hosick, 2020a) and the adoption of the NCAA's one-time transfer waiver rule has created a logjam where there are many more players with college basketball talent than there are scholarship spots. According to the NCAA's website, the transfer waiver "applies only to students who transferred from another Division I school, not transfers from other NCAA divisions or schools outside the NCAA. The regular transfer waiver process is available to non-Division I transfer student-athletes" (Hosick, 2020b, para. 3)

This has created a merit-based lottery system where the cream of the crop prospects in terms of those who are viewed as having the potential to contribute right away to a team's success are receiving scholarship placements and others who may be viewed as needing some additional time to develop like high school prospects are being left out of athletic scholarship opportunities with increasing frequency. Some high school seniors who had stellar seasons and would ordinarily be recruited by major programs aren't getting scholarships offers from any school. Scholarship slots are just not in abundance.

The combination of NCAA rule changes and the COVID-19 pandemic has resulted in an intrusion that has upset the normal equilibrium of college athletics. The window of opportunity for change is open and it is the dawn of new era in college athletics for everyone involved.

Major adaptations will need to be incorporated as people adjust to the seismic changes that are taking place and will take place. One needed change that will hopefully be on the horizon is a shift away from a disproportionate reliance on the "athletic lottery". The traditional lottery where large amounts of money is awarded to a few lucky people does not have the same level of overreliance that the athletic lottery has. People in large part do not solely focus on winning that lottery. Those who play surely daydream about what it would be like to win, but they do not abandon other routes to success in the way that far too many young people do in their pursuit of careers in professional athletics.

Sports has long been a fixture in American life generally and in communities of color more specifically. One could argue that there is seemingly more at stake on average for Black athletes because of the economic condition of Black communities in the United States. The cultural embeddedness of the athletic route and the sports dream in the lives of young Black men is something that is taken for granted in many cases. For the small few who make it to play in college or the pros, a glimmer of hope for the masses is given.

There is no doubt that participation in sports does afford many young people opportunities that they may not have gotten if they did not play sports. An athletic scholarship can be a means to a college degree. The right degree gives them opportunities in the workforce even if it does not lead to being a professional athlete. An argument can be made, however, that these same student-athletes could have garnered similar opportunities if they were pushed towards academic endeavors with an equivalent level of intensity and celebration that is often attached to sports.

There is no harm in young people going after their sports dreams, but they should be made aware of the lottery like aspect of the process. Their dream athletic program will likely only sign one or two players at their position out of the entire World. This reality hits too many prospective college student-athletes too late. Too many have ignored or neglected their academic development in favor of going all in on their aspiration to play at the highest level of college athletics.

This is the time to utilize the crisis that some student-athletes are going through in terms of not getting the recruitment that they anticipated to intervene in their lives and shift the culture for the student-athletes who will be coming behind them. This shake up of the athletic lottery can be a catalyst to cause student-athletes who were previously limiting themselves to only seeking fulfillment and purpose in the athletic realm to understand that they can go hard and achieve excellence both in sports and in the classroom.

The Athletic Identity

Student-athletes all have some level of investment in their particular sport. This investment can come in the form of effort, time, emotions, money, hopes, and dreams. Perhaps the most impactful investment that they make is the investment of their identity. This is the level of which one's view of their self is defined as being an athlete in their sport. How people define themselves and how others define them makes up their identity.

Athletes can face a crossroads when the thing that they were hanging onto, the athletic career, is gone. They can go from being celebrated to not even acknowledged after their eligibility has expired or their formal participation as player in college sports has ended. There can be a scramble to find their place in the World. A person's athletic identity investment depends on their individual valuation of the importance of being considered an athlete and how much of their identity is based on it. It varies from person to person. What is meaningful to one person may not have any meaning at all to another.

The COVID-19 pandemic may have accelerated an identity crisis in people depending on their level of athletic identity investment. All sports and sporting experiences were altered to some extent by the pandemic. Some seasons were cancelled altogether while others were delayed. They all had some level of restricted fan access to view the games. In several college sports, student-athletes were able to play their seasons without losing a year of eligibility as they normally would. This combined with the implementation of the recent one-time transfer waiver rule where student-athletes are allowed to transfer without sitting out a year, has created many more available student-athletes for the same number of scholarship spots (Hosick, 2020b).

The inevitable consequence of this will be many prospective student-athletes who would usually sign college scholarships not having the opportunity to and then either not playing at all or playing at other levels of college athletics that may not have been their initial desire. This could potentially be devastating to individuals who had an elevated level of their identity investment in being a college athlete.

Some key questions are how much of the value that they see in themselves is predicated on the approval or external valuation of them by coaches and recruiting services? Have they bought into the narrative that sports are their only vehicle of social mobility? How much of their identity and elevated status is attached to being an athlete?

This predicament presents both challenges and opportunities for the student-athletes themselves and the many others who help to groom them at various levels of their development. Many athletes go into an unspoken, undiagnosed, and untreated depression after they have seen something that they invested their life into disappoint them. At that point the game and those who were attached to the game can become resented and even hated. If there is not adequate mental and psychological preparation, then problems will occur that could have been avoided.

Too many young people are being lost to a broken spirit and a shattered identity after their playing careers are over. The identity crisis that can occur at the end of formal competitive athletics should be anticipated, planned for, and proactively acted on. Colleges and universities should not just discard individuals after their playing careers are over.

The "more than an athlete" mantra should have feet to it and take student-athletes different places to discover new ways to be their best selves. It is an opportunity to introduce and emphasize other routes and potential passions. It is an opportunity to highlight some of the potential returns on all of their athletic investment.

In basketball the use of a "pivot" is one that prepares a person to move effectively in any direction. Being prepared to pivot and not being locked into one position or posture is a key to success on the court and in life. The ball will stop bouncing for everyone at some point. There should be a structured and regimented way to transfer the traits and characteristics that produced athletic success into other endeavors.

The skills and transferrable features that were cultivated over all of those years playing a particular sport should not be dead and buried at the conclusion of one's playing career. The setback of losing one's status and position as an athlete should be a setup to pivot into other areas where they can achieve even greater things. The ability to read defenses and put together strategies to counter them is transferrable. Being able to see and anticipate traps is transferable. Leading and motivating your teammates is transferrable.

Battling through adversity and coming back from significant odds is transferrable. Gracefully handling being demoted or going from a starting to a reserve role without losing your enthusiasm for the game or the team is transferrable. Changing positions or even playing outside of your "natural" position for the benefit of the team is good training for what goes on in the world of work and is transferrable. Accepting critical feedback in the moment and producing results in a highly competitive environment is transferrable.

This moment is an opportunity to create new habits and patterns before the old ones automatically kick back in by default as things move back towards "normal". This is a chance to examine regularity and make some needed adjustments. It is an opportunity to break out of the limited one-dimensional paradigm that so many people are locked into based on cultural embeddedness and athletic identity investment. It is an opportunity to transform how student-athletes view themselves.

A shift in mindset is the first step towards seeing a shift in behavior. When individuals change their actions and patterns then it can have a ripple effect on communities and regions. This is key to helping so many young people avoid having their broken sports dreams derail them from achieving their aspirations in other areas of life. This is the kind of paradigm shift that can happen if this inflection point in the world of college athletics is used in a transformational way.

Athletic Symbols

Symbols can have a great deal of impact on how a person identifies themselves with being an athlete. There are a number of symbolic elements that play a significant role in the institutionalization of the athletic lottery. Athletes from a particular area who make it into the professional ranks can become a symbol for many others who hope to follow in their footsteps. One example is Kenny Anderson in New York City.

The documentary "Mr. Chibbs" took a deep dive into Anderson's story. It served as both a biographical sketch of Anderson and a cautionary tale of the less glamorous side of fame and fortune. Anderson was incredibly transparent in the film about some of his past mistakes and demons that he admittedly still deals with. This kind of transparency is need for both current and former athletes to gain important insight about how to navigate their own journeys.

Elements of Anderson's journey can be seen in men young and old in almost every city. While Anderson's story is uniquely his, it is representative of some common themes that play out frequently in the world of athletics. Anderson was renowned in New York City for basketball since he was in the 6th grade. He was arguably the most heralded high school player since Lew Alcindor. Talented basketball and football players are often highly sought after in inner cities across the country by AAU travel teams and private schools.

Athletic talent is frequently utilized as a ticket to private high schools that are located both in their home city and in other parts of the country. This increases the incentive for children and parents to place an even greater emphasis on the development of athletic talent in hopes that it will create opportunities to attend better resourced high schools that can provide a higher level of academic instruction and athletic exposure.

Anderson's private school tuition at Archbishop Molloy High School was taken care of because of his exceptional ability to play basketball. Anderson described basketball as saving him from being the streets and doing wrong. It was his "sanctuary".

He followed in the footsteps of former University of North Carolina and NBA Player Kenny Smith. Smith hailed from the same LeFrak City neighborhood in Queens, NY as Anderson and served as an example of where basketball stardom could take you.

This also plays out in cities all over the country where certain players inspire a generation of younger players to follow their journey. Community adulation is even more prevalent when a native of their neighborhood makes it into the professional ranks. This is the ever-present dream that dominates the mind of urban athletes. Examples of players who had this kind of impact on their home areas are Isiah Thomas in Chicago, Anfernee "Penny" Hardaway in Memphis, and Dwayne "Pearl" Washington in New York City.

Anderson won the "Athletic Lottery" in the sense that his basketball ability allowed him to have access to one of the very few available slots in big time Division I basketball and the NBA. It is important to understand that making it to these levels of basketball is a lottery-like system because of the few opportunities available in comparison to the millions of people who are vying for these slots. The odds of getting there are slim to none regardless of one's desire to get there.

Many kids have the illusion of there being a much greater likelihood that they will reach the professional ranks than they have. The reality of many central cities creates a sense of urgency in many student-athletes where they feel that their lives will be cut short or will be lackluster if they don't escape the environment where they were raised. Anderson spoke about the struggles that his family went through during his early childhood years, including getting evicted and not having anywhere to go.

The importance of having alternative plans in place outside of athletics is one that should be emphasized to aspiring athletes in order to successfully navigate life when the deck is often stacked against them. Anderson went on to play collegiately at Georgia Tech and stated that he didn't want to leave school but couldn't pass on being a top NBA draft pick after being named as a first-team All American after his sophomore season. He ended up being selected as the number two pick in the 1991 NBA Draft.

Anderson had a solid first few years in the NBA including an All-Star Selection. He then became somewhat of an NBA journeyman playing for 9 different teams over the course of his career. He admitted during the film that his work ethic was adversely affected by money and fame and that excessive alcohol use also impeded his performance.

Additionally, Anderson's journey in the NBA serves as a cautionary tale of how to deal with outside influences including friends and family after making it to the NBA. Anderson outlined how he allowed his friends and families to raid his financial resources during and after his NBA career. This has also been a common theme for professional athletes. The ESPN 30 for 30 documentary "Broke" outlined this epidemic extensively.

The onslaught of requests and people that surround NBA draftees can undoubtedly be overwhelming. As Anderson stated in the film, "the more money, the more bills." He made over $60 million dollars in his playing career only to file for bankruptcy in 2005. He lived an extravagant lifestyle and generously gave his friends and family large sums of money. He stated during the film that "no one stole my money…I spoiled my mother to death….I didn't know how to say no".

Anderson is also representative of the plethora of athletes who have a multitude of kids by different women. The increased availability of women that sports and entertainment stardom brings can be difficult for some to handle. The film explores some of the relationships between Anderson and his children. He was open about his efforts to try to establish a better relationship with his children, particularly those who harbor an elevated level of resentment toward him.

The film also displays the identity crisis that he endured after his professional basketball career concluded. This is somewhat common for former athletes who struggle to find a sense of purpose after having invested so much into their given sport. The film begs the questions as to what happens to players after their pro careers. Many have difficulty dealing with their own self-perception after being defined as an athlete for the majority of their lives.

What do they do after their athletic pinnacle? How can they better transition into other areas of life? Anderson stated during the documentary that for him "basketball is easy, life is hard." Many former players feel lost after their playing careers are over. His story is also in alignment with so many young men who have their hoop dreams shattered after playing in high school or college. Some never get over the disappointment.

Hoop Dreams

There has perhaps been no greater depiction of the chase for the athletic lottery than aforementioned "Hoop Dreams" documentary. Documentaries like this have chronicled the journeys of aspiring young athletes as they strive to realize their athletic goals.

The documentary "Hoop Dreams" followed the journey of two student-athletes, Arthur Agee and William Gates, who initially went to the private St. Joseph's High School in suburban Westchester, Illinois on partial basketball scholarships after previous attending inner city Chicago Public Schools. Like Isiah Thomas before them, both Arthur and William make a three hour round trip each day from the city to the school.

St. Joseph's Basketball Coach Gene Pingatore frequently

referred to Isiah Thomas throughout the film when talking about Gates. The expectation for him to be the next Isiah Thomas is a clear theme. The film opens with Isiah Thomas, a Chicago native and NBA All Star for the Detroit Pistons, being introduced at the NBA All Star Game that was being played at Chicago Stadium.

The film shows Thomas on the screen and then shows Agee and Gates on the playground. Thomas is the embodiment of the dream. Agee would go on to adopt the nickname "Tuss" because he heard that Isiah's nickname used to be Tuss. He painted Tuss on his shoes. His bedroom walls were plastered with articles about and posters of Isiah Thomas.

Gates was a highly developed as a player as a freshman and was highly touted as one of the Chicagoland area's best players. He was a starter on the varsity team and had a stellar freshman season. Sportswriter Bill Gleason referred to Gates as the next Isiah Thomas when talking about him as a freshman. Gates was also pushed by his older brother Curtis. Curtis was a former high school basketball star who had success at Colby Junior College in Kansas before eventually quitting the team when he had transferred to the University of Central Florida. He was then banking of William to make it to the professional level to potentially fulfill the dream that he once had. Curtis says in the movie that "all these basketball dreams I had, they're gone. All my dreams are in him now. I want him to make it so bad I don't know what to do.".

Curtis went on to describe his free fall in "status" by saying that "I'm used to everybody in the neighborhood loving me and knowing how good I could play. It seemed like everyone looked up to me when I was playing basketball. Now, I'm just a regular old guy on the streets now." Curtis is representative of millions of other Black men who feel like or find themselves in the same predicament. Agee had not yet hit his growth spurt and lingered on the freshman team.

At the second half of the academic year, the school found a sponsor who would cover the full amount of Gates tuition for the entirety of his career there. Agee and his family were left with a bill that showed an unpaid balance and prevented them from registering for any additional classes. The news came at a particularly bad time for the Agee family as his father, Bo Agee, was struggling to maintain employment. He expressed his frustration saying that he had "worked for Sara Lee, got laid off. Worked for Scholars Meat Packing, got laid off. You look around your house and you see the bills getting low. Bill due here, bill due there." With the Agee's owing $1,500 in back payments. Arthur was forced to leave the school.

Arthur described the situation as he saw it by saying "I guess he (Pingatore) thought 'well he is not going to be that big of a ball player so why would I waste money on him." Arthur was describing the transactional nature of basketball at elevated levels. He was treated as disposable when he was not seen to be a basketball asset.

Arthur's Mom, Shelia, articulated the impact that this had on her son's mindset by saying "he was so depressed and devastated that he just closed himself off in his room. I told him, hey, things will look up." Her comments suggest the depth of the level of Agee's identity that was tied to his basketball trajectory.

At the beginning of Gates' and Agee's junior year they seemed to be going in different trajectories with Gates being heavily recruited by major basketball programs from across the country and the financial condition of Agee's family worsening.

Arthur's mom, Shelia, described their situation by saying "now I'm on welfare that I wasn't on then and trying to live month to month on something like that is very hard. And you have three kids that need this and that, it's just not enough to make ends meet.....I was cut off for three months....Our lights were cut off, our gas was cut off, and we were sitting in the dark."

William suffers an injury during the preseason of his junior year in practice that sidelines him for most of the season. This highlights the capriciousness of the athletic lottery. An injury can derail one's entire career and future trajectory for what level of the athletic lottery they ascend it. William also had a baby daughter during his junior year raising the stakes of his athletic lottery chase even more.

William's injury shook his entire family who also had a deep level of investment in his dream. His mother, Emma Gates, said after his injury "I really thought Curtis was going to make it, but he didn't make it so I just wanted this one to make it." William weighed in on Curtis' attitude towards him saying "it was like my injury was making him look bad. I always felt that Curtis should not be living his dream through me."

Curtis is shown making a painting a picture of what William's future may be if he doesn't hit the athletic lottery. "When basketball is over William may not have a friend in the world.....Sometimes I just sit around and my eyes just get watery because I'm just like I ain't amount to nothing, I ain't got nothing. I can't even get a job making 7 dollars an hour. I tell myself, you ain't gone get no better." This happened after Curtis was laid off from a security guard job and couldn't find a job for 4 months.

William quipped "people say, 'when you make it to the NBA,

don't forget about me.' I feel like telling them, 'Well, if I don't make it, make sue you don't forget about me." Eventually Curtis was able to get a job through Patricia Weir, William's financial sponsor at St. Joseph's High School. This was an early family benefit from the athletic lottery and Curtis acknowledges it as such saying "I was out of work for about a year. If it weren't for William knowing Ms. Weir I wouldn't be here… That's the first thing I saw when I walked in the door, not hiring… It's about as good as a person without a college degree can do so I feel like I'll be here for a while."

This highlights the importance of the social capital needed to open up economic doors that is too often lacking in the lives of people of color. The athletic lottery frequently gives one an elevated level of social capital for a certain window of time. It is up to the athlete to maximize the window of opportunity will the opportunity to maximize is available. Unfortunately, a significant segment of society regards Black men as disposable after they can no longer serve an athletic purpose.

Arthur's career takes an upturn after making the varsity team at Marshall High School and breaking into the starting lineup. The role of basketball takes on an additional level of importance as he encounters multiple levels of adversity off the court. In addition to the families' financial struggles there are two new members of the Agee household. His sister had a baby and his best friend Shannon moved in to escape his own troubled home.

It is at this point where the role of the underground drug economy asserts itself in a prominent way in Agee's life with his father becoming a drug addict and his best friend becoming a drug dealer. It was likely Agee's hoop dreams and athletic lottery hopes that steered him away from going down one of those paths even when those who were close to him and many others did.

The late rapper the Notorious B.I.G. as was referred to earlier in this book summed it up his predicament in his song "Things Done Changed" when he said "the streets is a short stop, either you're slingin' crack rock or you got a wicked jump shot." There is a scene where Arthur's dad shows up to a playground where Arthur is playing basketball during the summer after his sophomore year. The movie's narrator says that the playground had increasingly become a place to buy and sell drugs. Arthur sees his father going to the other side of the court to buy drugs.

His father, Bo, would end up serving seven months in prison before overcoming his addiction to crack cocaine. He would rejoin the family after being released from prison and the movie displays him rededicating himself to Christ and becoming very involved in their church. Arthur remains skeptical. He would later reflect on this period with his father saying "when I was little you know, he had let me down. People were coming up to me saying that your Dad is on drugs. I remember when he would try to go to church when he was still on drugs.". His father recognized his son's skepticism and hesitancy by speaking on his son's mindset towards him at the time and him probably wondering "am I just doing this now or am I going to break bad again"?.

His best friend Shannon would eventually drop out of school, sell drugs, and get arrested. An unfortunate cycle of events that had fed the "school-to-prison pipeline" for too many people for too many years. The lure of quick money in the drug game can be too much for many to resist. Both Arthur and Shannon got a taste of the potential financial benefits of drug trafficking. A scene in the movie shows them both buying shoes and athletic gear from money that they had gotten from drug dealers in the neighborhood. Shannon remarked that "some of the drug pushers in the neighborhood, they give us money and tell us to go shop and get you something. They think that if we are playing basketball, then they can give us stuff and keep our career going. That's how we really keep up with the styles."

The film ends with William eventually recovering from his injury and Agee resurrecting his high school basketball career at Marshall High School and being an intricate part of the team's state tournament run. Both were athletic lottery recipients at the collegiate level with Gates going to Marquette University on a basketball scholarship and Agee getting basketball scholarships to Mineral Area Junior College and Arkansas State University.

Gates selects Marquette after being told that by the head coach that he is one of seven guys that they were recruiting. "Seven guys for 3 spots" remarked then Coach Kevin O'Neill to Gates. Some of the other schools that were recruiting him postponed their planned visits for him preferring to see how William would do during his senior year after he again hurt his knee during the Nike All-American Camp that took place during the summer between his junior and senior season.

Arthur's grades prevented him from being eligible for a Division I college basketball scholarship so going the junior college route was the option for him. A junior college coach that was at one of Arthur's games described his situation and the predicament of many others by saying "a lot of these kids won't talk to a Junior College until they see the dream of Illinois, UNLV, Indiana start to fade."

Arthur's mom, Shelia, expressed pride with Arthur's progression and his opportunity to continue his education and basketball career at the next level after going through the adversity that he was able to overcome. "I never thought that he would get to the place where he is now. Arthur's self-esteem was really drained from St. Joseph's. I said you are somebody. No matter where you go, it is in your heart that you are really going to go somewhere."

William's mother gave him the same kind of encouragement when he was preparing to depart for Marquette as William recalls her saying "everyone is throwing their dreams into you, but you have to throw your own dreams into yourself." This is reflective of the transferability of hoop dreams and how the dreams can somehow continue vicariously through other people in addition to one's own individual dream.

Athletes May Be the Key to Advancing Dr. King's Final Campaign

Dr. Martin Luther King Jr. explicitly spoke about leveraging the economic power of people and using it strategically to accomplish aims during his last speech at the Mason Temple in Memphis, Tennessee on the night of April 3, 1968. He urged the crowd to "always anchor our external direct action with the power of economic withdrawal." He called for boycotts of specific companies because of their hiring practices and lack of support for the movement to improve the working conditions and pay of Black sanitation workers in the city.

It was a part of a larger "Poor People's Campaign" that would be the last of Dr. King's life. His final years were spent making a very aggressive push towards economic justice. College athletes can play a major in this as they are social justice sleeping giants who have a tremendous amount of potential power that they can leverage on their campuses, surrounding areas, and hometowns to create positive change. They can the key catalysts in reinvigorating the momentum behind Dr. King's final campaign and paving the way for the economic transformation of America.

King differentiated this economic push from previous ones by indicating that this one would be more difficult because it would ultimately cost the nation more. He said as much in a 1966 article in "The Nation" when he wrote that "Negroes have benefitted from a limited change that was emotionally satisfying but materially deficient...Jobs are harder to create than voter rolls" (King, 1966).

Economically empowering communities is a multilayered process. The need for governmental intervention is clear. Government policies and implementation played an overwhelming role in creating present-day economic disparities and they need to play the same kind of role in reversing them. There is also a need for education and opportunity creation in areas like financial literacy, investing, cryptocurrencies, real estate, entrepreneurship, and the like.

Both personal and social responsibility are relevant and important factors in creating positive economic change. Operationalizing and making real the ideals that institutions, governments, and other entities proclaim will not happen without the strategic leveraging of the power that groups of people have.

Pooling and leveraging the power that historically excluded groups have in areas like sports and entertainment can be a gamechanger in terms of pushing policies and practices that can produce tangible economic benefits, especially for those who have been left out of the financial prosperity that America has to offer. Athletes can organize and use their elevated social status to be a vehicle to empower themselves and unlock the economic gates of opportunity for their broader communities.

Sports Stars Have an Obligation to Continue the Fight for Social Equity and Justice

The recent tragedies and controversies over several racially tinged incidents have created a conundrum for many people who don't usually speak out about issues of race and inequality. Everyone from Michael Jordan to people in general workplaces have been vocal in a way that they weren't before. Many people are deciding if they should weigh in and if so, to what extent. How discrete or "politically correct" should they be? What will happen if their employer finds out that they are engaged in protests about a controversial issue?

There is a history of individuals paying a severe career price for engaging in the movement for civil rights and there has been a heightened level of acceptance and reward in the upper echelons of many industries and institutions for those who are perceived as docile and non-threatening. This may explain the relative silence of many athletes who may believe that speaking out will jeopardize potentially lucrative career opportunities like endorsement deals. If they muster up the courage to outwardly fight for justice within their workplace and outside of it, then they may be risking the employment that financially provides for themselves and their families.

Ministers, like those associated with the Southern Christian Leadership Conference (SCLC), were historically at the forefront of the civil rights movement in large part because their economic base came from their congregations and not traditional employers. This gave them the freedom to speak their minds with minimal negative financial consequences.

Several athletes have garnered a fortune that puts them on an exclusive socioeconomic island far away from the masses of minorities who often live in communities characterized by economic deprivation and poverty. A report from the Institute of Policy Studies noted that it would take 228 years for the average Black family to have the same net worth as their White counterparts (Asante-Muhammed et al., 2016).

The wealth and platform that these athletes have amassed affords them a financial independence similar to that of the aforementioned ministers. A sense of a broader responsibility should come with this status as they are the beneficiaries of the sacrifices made by those who came before them.

Modern day athletes and everyday professionals are frequently told that they would be committing career suicide by engaging in civil rights and to stay away from social activism so as not to be seen as too militant or radical. The punishment for stepping outside of the box and speaking out can be severe. Muhammed Ali had to make incredible career sacrifices for being vocal about his beliefs and being critical of U.S. foreign policy in Vietnam. His stances and refusal to be inducted into the army ultimately cost him his prime fighting years. He was a different fighter when he finally returned to the ring.

The sacrifices that were made by Ali and others like Jim Brown and Bill Russell is ultimately what made them legendary figures. The fortune and fame that many athletes have garnered should not just be an end, but it can be used as a platform to advance equity and social justice. They have a special opportunity to shine a light on issues that need to be publicized. NBA stars LeBron James, Dwayne Wade, Carmelo Anthony, and Chris Paul did an admirable job of highlighting important concerns during the ESPY Awards in 2016 and other athletes like have very solid records of community involvement. Hopefully, their actions will inspire more of their peers to increase their level of engagement with social issues.

The next step beyond bringing awareness to certain issues is to identify and promote specific policy measures that would move the ball forward. Athletes don't necessarily have to be policy wonks on their issues of choice, but they can use their leverage to bring key people to the table where big decisions are made. They can help to start key conversations with policymakers and bring along a coalition with them to help complete them. College and professional athletes can also exercise influence within their own arena by using their leverage to create off the court opportunities for minorities who have been previously locked out of certain areas.

The stance that the University of Missouri football team took in 2015 in support of their fellow students who were protesting over racial issues on campus is an example of the kind of leverage and power that athletes can have. The movement at Mizzou prompted the resignation of the University of Missouri System President and caused universities across the country to reexamine their policies and practices related to diversity, equity, and inclusion on campus.

Additionally, high profile athletes can influence millions of young boys and girls to act in ways that are not just self-beneficial, but act in ways that benefit the greater good. The ability for young athletes to see themselves in others and to shun the status of being the typical socially uninvolved athletes can and should be cultivated. This message goes beyond athletes and expands to those who occupy more conventional occupations. This is the time for people to come out from behind their cubicles and push the envelope on issues that matter to them. Effective leadership is not in the center, it is on the edge.

When athletes take the risk to speak out, it can inspire the broader public to utilize their platform to advance important causes. People of all walks of life can be motivated to address the stratification of opportunity that remains in many communities. Sports figures can attack societal challenges with the same vigor and enthusiasm that they exhibit on the courts and playing fields and be Hall of Famers in making a positive influence in areas that desperately need to be uplifted.

Black Male Images and Narratives in the Media

There is a need to examine the narratives about Black males that have risen to prominence and have gained a foothold in the nation's psyche. The way that public policy is shaped and implemented is highly impacted by the narratives that are attached to the people who will be impacted by the legislation. Narratives that are advanced by the media help to shape public opinion and who is deemed as "deserving" of investment, support, and justice. Narratives play a major role in shaping both perception and reality and can be more powerful than scientific research in influencing how policy is designed and implemented.

The imagery of the Black male that is depicted in the media not only plays a big role in shaping the external narratives of how Black boys and men are seen, but it also impacts how they see themselves. These narratives can be internalized and affect both the way that people act and the way that they are treated. There can be a whole host of associations that are attached to individuals or groups based on stereotypes that are derived from derogatory narratives. The more that a narrative is repeated, the higher the likelihood is that it will be internalized and broadly disseminated.

The imagery of the Black male that is depicted in the media not only plays a big role in shaping the external narratives of how Black boys and men are seen, but it also impacts how they see themselves. These narratives can be internalized and affect both the way that people act and the way that they are treated. There can be a whole host of associations that are attached to individuals or groups based on stereotypes that are derived from derogatory narratives. The more that a narrative is repeated, the higher the likelihood is that it will be internalized and broadly disseminated.

Narratives have the power to lead to action. The understanding of how narratives are utilized is important because it gives insight into how issues may be viewed by policymakers and how they become important in the broader public. The media presents stories to the masses who may not know the different dynamics and context of a particular issue. There is a need to constantly examine the narratives about Black males that have been repeated so often that they are taken for granted.

Journalists can use their talent and platforms to shed light on different narratives that need an opportunity to compete for dominance. Negative narratives have to be challenged and contended against for them to be altered. It is difficult to change narratives that have been deeply embedded and institutionalized like many derogatory ones about Black males have been. There is a confrontation and battle that must take place to upend the status quo.

The nation is in need of a new Civil War. Not a war of guns and bullets, but a war of competing narratives. It must happen for transformative change to take place. The mission of this needed war is very similar to how Frederick Douglass described the mission of the Civil War in an 1864 speech that he gave to the Women's Loyal League at the Cooper Institute in New York City. Douglass proclaimed that "I do believe that it is the manifest destiny of this war to unify and reorganize the institutions of the country, and that herein is the secret of the strength, the fortitude, the persistent energy – in a word, the sacred significance of this war."

Before the Civil War was declared, there was a war of competing narratives about the role of slavery that was being waged through ideas, ideals, and stories. Douglass realized that there had to be a battle, a necessary struggle. Douglass was utilizing narratives to place the emancipation of Black people from physical bondage as the mission of the civil war.

The emancipation of Black people from economic, social, and political bondage as the mission of a needed narrative war that must take place for transformational progress to occur. In our present times like in the times of Frederick Douglass, an impasse and a war must occur for new narratives and new possibilities to overtake the existing realities and status quo narratives. There is a need for new narratives to achieve dominance and implementation both internally and externally. A battle of competing narratives is at the core of the public policymaking process.

Negative narratives about Black males in the media should not go unchallenged. If they do then these constructed images will become embedded, and the negative imagery will cause Black males to be excluded from important discussions about who resources should be directed to. The most meaningful and important narratives are the ones that people go to battle with. These are the ones that people live by and build their lives around. Successful narrative frameworks can be used as interstate highways to transport excellence from one area to another.

If more positive and empowering narratives are given more airtime and opportunities to compete against the existing negative narratives, then a great deal of them can potentially become dominant and get implemented into the hearts, minds, policies, practices, institutions, and cultures of the communities that make up the nation. People buy into winning narratives and implement them into their lives. They help to guide the direction of their thoughts and actions. Narratives also inform the mindsets behind how Black men are treated in classrooms, courtrooms, and board rooms over the course of their lives.

This day of focus on Black male narratives in the media can be expanded to a larger movement that can provide a sustained counter to the onslaught of negative imagery and depictions. One does not have to be locked into the existing narratives. They can be changed. New narratives can become dominant and cause new actions to displace old practices.

The power behind media narratives and what is consumed by the masses is extremely pivotal. Momentum can be created to flip scripts and rewrite narratives. Narratives can be used to advance progress and reshape the image and status of Black males. Positive imagery that is consistently projected in airwaves and media publications can be tapped into for the empowerment of those who are reflected. Narratives that were weaponized to limit Black males can be flipped and used to liberate them.

The Impact of Stereotypes

The extent to which Black athletes mirror basketball and football stereotypes as well as the extent to which Black men are treated based on stereotypes about them are also a part of the cultural-cognitive pillar. One reverse example that can be illustrative is the example of White cornerbacks in the NFL.

Cornerback is generally regarded as the position in the National Football League (NFL) where some of the fastest and most athletic players are placed. The position requires tremendous forward, backward, and lateral speed and quickness. It requires one to defend wide receivers that may have speed that approaches the level of Olympic track athletes.

The last White cornerback to start a game in the NFL was Jason Sehorn. Sehorn retired at the end of the 2003 season. Stereotypes certainly play a key role in this phenomenon. White players in some quarters are stereotyped as not having the requisite speed and quickness to be able to excel at the cornerback position. This likely prevents young White players from attempting to play the position, coaches from placing them in the position, and college recruiters from recruiting them to play the position.

The stereotype is so dominant that many young players likely remove themselves from the competition for spots before it even begins. This is an example of the kind of psychological consequences that deeply embedded stereotypes can have. It would be hard to gauge the internal and external impact of this stereotype on white players who aspire to play positions in the NBA and NFL that require elite foot speed in order to excel.

The plight of the White cornerback can shed light on the experience of minority groups in almost every other sector of society. There is a presumption of slowness for White players that exists in the minds of many. They often have their ability questioned more frequently and are scrutinized more harshly when competing for positions and playing time. These stereotypes represent powerful identity contingencies that aspiring White cornerbacks must face.

They are frequently typecast as just being suitable for certain positions like "shooters" in basketball and "linemen" in football. They usually have to go above and beyond to prove themselves worthy. Black athletes are often given the benefit of the doubt in the area of speed and quickness. Slower Black players are often perceived to be quicker than they really are. This represents an implicit bias in the minds of many towards Black players in the area of pure athleticism.

The paucity of White cornerbacks represents the reverse of almost every other area of the country including most institutions of higher education. The situation is flipped for the vast majority of domains in the rest of society. Black people, especially Black men, are often valued for athletics and entertainment, but little else. An argument can be made that several universities are examples of this.

Some of the numbers from a University of Pennsylvania report by Dr. Shaun Harper entitled "Black Male Student-Athletes and Racial Inequities in NCAA Division I College Sports" suggest that the primary recruitment mechanisms for black males may be their football and basketball teams for many universities. The report "found that black men were 2.8 percent of undergraduate students but 57.1 percent of football players and 64.3 percent of basketball players across the 77 major sports programs."

What if Black people were given the same benefit of the doubt and presumption of competence in other areas of life? What if there were more models of excellence in areas outside of sports and entertainment that were highlighted and celebrated? What if young scholars of color were pursued and recruited with the same intensity that prized athletes of color are?

Unfortunately for Blacks, professional careers in athletics represent an incredibly small percentage of the ways that people earn a living. In most other career paths, microaggressions, implicit bias, and negative stereotypes present significant barriers to progression.

Every day, doors of opportunity are opened or closed based on the stereotypes of one's particular group. It is like a shadow that follows people everywhere they go. These stereotypes often lead to people formulating particular expectations about students and/or faculty at colleges and universities can do and where they should be placed.

There has been a great deal of discussion about glass ceilings, but even more often minorities experience glass doors. They can't even get in the door when it comes to securing faculty positions for example, in spite of their Ph.Ds. Studies suggest that they have been locked out of high-level positions at many institutions of high education and other industries.

Like the White cornerback, minorities often face an increased level of scrutiny. They may have to be two or three times as qualified to get an opportunity. There may be limitations placed on how high they can go and how many of them are allowed access to certain roles.

These additional barriers combined with an environment that is sometimes discouraging can have a destructive impact. When they dare to bring these issues up, students and faculty of color are frequently subject to experience microinvalidations that are cumulative in nature. Microinvalidations are those times when their racial realities are dismissed, nullified, and negated. As a result, the issues are likely to never be addressed in a holistic manner.

Hopefully, the plight of White cornerbacks can shed light on the experience of minority groups in almost every other sector of society. The blueprint to broaden avenues of access, diversity, and inclusion exists in basketball and football. It needs to be utilized for other areas of life.

PART 2: THE ROLE OF TECH

Finding brighter ways forward in the area of tech is critical because there are many indicators that suggest that it will represent a sizable portion of the future of the economy. Accelerating in higher wage sectors like tech is imperative for people who are significantly less likely to be the recipients of sizable inter-generational wealth transfers and exposure to opportunity for transformational socioeconomic mobility.

They are often in the social and economic marketplace having to make it with their individual connections and income against others who are much more likely to have multiple generations of social capital and funneled down financial wealth that they can add to their own to make purchases like housing, cars, college, and investments.

The main portion of part two will be a series of "Inspiring Tech" essays that will focus on inspiring tech dreams, discipline, bridges, pipelines, economics, participation, and on-ramps. These will all represent brighter ways forward to creating an environment where people can flourish within the tech sector and enhance the quality of life of themselves and their communities through the opportunities that are connected to it.

A Laser Focus on Math is Needed to Diversify the STEM Pipeline

The common denominator for entry into most STEM (Science, Technology, Engineering, and Mathematics) majors is the ability to successfully complete high level math courses. There is no getting around the requirement of these classes to obtain degrees in majors like engineering, computer science, and chemistry. There may not be one magic bullet to increase the diversity of students in STEM majors but placing a laser-like focus on academic achievement in mathematics will help more students get past gatekeeper courses like Calculus.

Universities can design and/or expand summer bridge programs that focus extensively on building competency in mathematics for students who are interested in majoring in STEM fields, but lack a strong math background. They can also dedicate funding streams to support summer school learning opportunities for current students who need to catch up on math courses in order to stay on track to graduate within four years.

An accelerated level of peer-to-peer tutoring opportunities and other wrap around support services would also be helpful in these efforts. It will ultimately be up to the students to take the initiative to utilize these services. Students must cultivate the will and desire to help them get over the roadblocks that they will inevitably encounter in these courses. They need a consistent support system to encourage them to dig deeper.

Many students doubt themselves and lack confidence in their ability to successfully complete higher level math classes. These feelings cause some to give up on majors like engineering before they even begin. There should be efforts to build an academic swagger in them from an early age to help overcome the barriers that they may set for themselves.

There are an assortment of partnerships and varying mechanisms of engagement that higher education institutions have with K-12 educational systems. Most engagement of any kind should be applauded and supported. There is, however, a need to strategically target these efforts. Some colleges and universities have random and sporadic engagement that may not be focused on the most pivotal areas of need.

A lot of the programming in the area of STEM seems to be around the area of general exposure. This is crucial and is very much needed to help generate awareness of STEM careers for students who may not be aware of certain occupational avenues but generating interest without helping to develop the required math competency is a losing formula.

In the realm of education at the secondary school level, there is also a need to put an extra focus on achievement in mathematics. All subjects in school have value and are generally worthy of study. Young people should strive to make A's in every subject. Unfortunately, too many students underachieve in classes beyond basic Algebra. These courses end up being stumbling blocks that many students don't seem to get past.

The consequence of this is that the choice of majoring in a high growth STEM field when they reach a college or university is taken off of the table due to a lack of math competency. The long-term impact of this is a furthering of an occupational segregation that cloisters large numbers of minorities into lower wage occupations.

There is additionally a tremendous need for highly qualified and motivated math teachers at the elementary school level.

Different models for increased compensation may need to be explored to attract the most competent and capable math teachers into classrooms. There is a premium on talented educators who can effectively disseminate information and instruction that is connected to tangible careers. It is important for the real-world application of abstract mathematical concepts to be explicitly highlighted and reinforced.

Communities can also assist with placing an enhanced priority on high-level math achievement. Higher education institutions can assist community organizations with creating avenues for people who have expertise in these subjects to convey their knowledge to students. This can occur at after-school programs, sports camps, and summer activities hosted by universities or other entities. This exposure and support can be a spark and motivating force for students to apply themselves more to master higher level math content.

If colleges and universities are sincere about increasing the diversity of the students who are entering STEM majors, then they must leverage their capacity and expertise to increase the math competency of their prospective and current students. Institutions should continue to devise ways to cultivate the keys to open the mathematical gates that prevent many students of color from graduating with degrees in STEM fields.

The Importance of Early and Consistent Exposure to STEM Fields

The lack of minorities in STEM (science, technology, engineering, and mathematics) occupations has been well-documented (10 Startling Stats About Minorities in STEM, 2016). A 2015 article by Mother Jones suggested that the combined Black workforce at Google, Twitter and Facebook could fit into a large plane (Harkinson, 2015). The National Science Foundation found that the STEM workforce is no more diverse than it was 14 years ago (Shepherd, 2016).

The combination of an inept outreach to HBCUs and other producers of qualified STEM workers and a lack of large numbers of people of color in the STEM pipeline have contributed to where we are. This highlights and underscores a need for more exposure for students at the K-12 level. An increased level of early exposure will help to make the requisite math courses needed for many STEM careers more relevant to students. Critical math courses are often criticized by students as being too abstract and not relevant to the real world.

It is also important for college students who are in STEM majors to get consistent exposure to opportunities in the STEM economy. This will likely increase the level of persistence in majors that have traditionally seen high levels of attrition. Minority students are more likely to change their majors after they are enrolled in a STEM major (10 Startling Stats About Minorities in STEM, 2016).

A broader early exposure to STEM careers would also aid in the creation of a tiered job entry system. Not all jobs in the STEM sector require advanced degrees or even bachelor's degrees. An increased awareness of positions like radiology specialists and network specialists will create entry points for a broader population of people into the STEM world.

Formal connections and partnerships between STEM companies and schools need to be established and expanded. This will help to encourage K-12 and postsecondary educational institutions to more closely align their curriculum and instructional techniques to match the quickly evolving needs of sectors where great job growth is predicted.

Cities and municipalities should create incentives for employer engagement with schools. Elected officials can play a key part in recruiting STEM employers to urban communities and to appropriate resources to ensure that residents are prepared for careers in these fields. Companies that employ large numbers of STEM workers can also provide avenues of training and employment to the long-term unemployed and underrepresented minorities.

Early and consistent exposure to STEM professionals of color will also help to reduce the stereotype threat that is often associated with garnering the knowledge, skills and abilities to gain access to STEM occupations. The stereotype threat has to deal with the thought process behind Blacks and other minorities not being able to succeed in higher-level math courses that are required to earn degrees in majors like engineering. Researchers Claude Steele and Joshua Aronson defined stereotype threat as "the risk of confirming negative stereotypes about an individual's racial, ethnic, gender, or cultural group" ("Stereotype Threat," 2013).

There should also be incentives created for the establishment of apprenticeship programs. These kinds of programs are critical to providing exposure and opportunities to those who may not have a natural connection into these companies.

The status quo of an extreme underrepresentation of minorities in STEM fields and occupations must be resisted against with a concentrated effort for greater inclusion. We must come out of our traditional silos to create more access to the jobs of the future by bolstering intentional connections between employers, school districts and higher education institutions.

The S.T.E.M. Pipeline Test: Will Underrepresented Groups Be Left at the Station as the Tech Train Takes Off?

Years of talking about and organizing around diversifying the science, technology, engineering, and mathematics (S.T.E.M.) pipeline is about to be put to the test immediately in cities like Miami. The tech train is leaving the station and while it is wonderful for those who will be on the board with lucrative economic opportunities it may further marginalize those who are left back at the station of occupational segregation and economic stratification.

684 high paying tech-orientated jobs with an average salary of $162,000 a year are headed to downtown Miami with more to come (The Next Miami, 2021). The push to bring Silicon Valley to Miami has accelerated significantly during the Covid-19 pandemic due a number of factors including the expansion of the virtual workplace which enabled people to work from anywhere, no state taxes, and a year-round warm climate. Additional efforts lead by City of Miami Mayor Francis Suarez in recruiting tech companies to the city have helped to intensify the pace of their arrival.

The big changes in the tech sector that are happening in Miami can be scary for some. There is a fear of being left behind and not being able to keep up with or afford the "New Miami". There are fears that this will accelerate the pace of some unwanted elements of what has taken place in areas like San Francisco for some time like massively overpriced housing, crippling traffic, and a reduced overall quality of life. There is concern that the bulk of the population will be in Bedrock living like the stone age "Flintstones" while the other part of town will be living in the space age like the "Jetsons". Will kids who are currently growing up in Miami be able to afford to live in the city when they reach adulthood?

The influx of tech companies represents an intrusion into the Miami economy that has brought about a moment of impasse where maintaining the status quo could result in an even greater bifurcation of social classes. The question of how equitable the New Miami will be remains to be seen. The bill for the S.T.E.M. push that has taken place for a number of years now is due in Miami and the pending question is how diverse the payment will be. Will underrepresented communities get a piece of this pie or be left with crumbs that are pushed off of the "big table"? Who is in the pipeline and prepared to take advantage of this window of opportunity?

Equity and justice in access to opportunity is something that stakeholders will have to be vigilant around if some of the mistakes of the past are to be avoided. Rapid progress in the tech space will not be accompanied by equity unless intentional efforts are made to provide access to digital tools, skills training, and a cutting-edge curriculum that will empower people to gain access to the tech prosperity train.

We must find immediate ways to build bridges to connect people with these emerging opportunities. Bridges need to be constructed to close the tech opportunity divide without delay. There is a crucial need to align the skills needed in the increasing digitization of the economy with the training that takes place on a regular basis.

A race to train the people who already exist in the area for these new tech positions should be pursued with the same intensity that firms and people are being recruited to come to Miami. It is not too late to connect more people with new pathways to get on the train before it leaves the station. New pathways to skill development are a primary component to the kind of social transformation that can occur for those who are able to get aboard and ride the tech train.

As daunting as it may seem to some, the influx of tech-oriented companies that are coming to Miami and other cities across the country is something that should be faced head on and embraced. This movement is not something that can be run from but is something that we should run towards. A new narrative about technology that informs people's day-to-day meaning system needs to become dominant to the point where standard practices change.

There are certainly great challenges, particularly in the areas of equity, access, and inclusion but they can be met with strategic partnerships and collaboration to provide pathways of opportunity. College and universities look to be the key connecting institutions between lucrative jobs and populations that have historically been unable to take advantage of previous economic booms.

There is also a need for higher education institutions to partner with employers to provide work experiences that will be designed to enable students to gain exposure to the requirements of the tech working world and to be inspired and energized to continue their studies through the practical application of their skills and knowledge. New bridges are needed to connect diverse students with the emerging tech field. The window of opportunity is open and the S.T.E.M. pipeline test is here. The tech train is about to leave the station. Whether or not we get on board is up to us.

Inspiring Tech Dreams

The challenge of diversity, equity, and inclusion in emerging tech sectors in cities across the country is multifaceted. This is especially the case when comes to creating avenues to make employment and entrepreneurship opportunities accessible and attainable for underrepresented populations.

There is a need for new "tech dreams" to inspire people to be motivated to take advantage of some of the structures of opportunity that are being constructed by higher education institutions, corporations, school systems, and other entities. Structures without the requisite level of student motivation can lead to hollow victories and superficial progress when it comes to expanding economic inclusion and opportunity.

The early 1990s movie *Hoop Dreams* depicted the stories of two young men from Chicago, Arthur Agee and William Gates, and their pursuit of making it to the upper echelons of basketball achievement. Their story is a microcosm of the kind of sports dreams that millions of young people have and aspire to fulfill.

Both young men had a figure that embodied the role that they wanted to fulfill in Isiah Thomas. Thomas was the embodiment of their respective Hoop dreams. They both played the guard position like Thomas and began their high school careers making the three-hour roundtrip commute from the west side of Chicago to the private St. Joseph's High School in Westchester, Illinois. Examples like Thomas in basketball, who was an NBA All Star and World Champion with the Detroit Pistons, can be identified, introduced, and promoted in other fields like technology as well.

Thomas was visible proof that their dream could be actualized by someone who came from the same neighborhood and circumstances that they came from. Some of the elements that are used to produce sports dreams can be utilized to generate "tech dreams". There are tech professionals who are operating at a high level in their field who can be symbols for individuals who aspire to have careers in technology. Students can be inspired to generate their own tech dreams like Agee and Gates had hoop dreams. For that to happen opportunities need to be made plain and repeatedly presented to populations that have historically received limited access and exposure to tech sector career pathways.

It is hard to aspire to be a part of something that you are unfamiliar with. It is hard to begin with the end in mind when you don't know what the end looks like. The day-to-day reality of what tech professionals do is vague for many. It needs to be made plain so individuals can have a clear vision of what they are aiming for. People need to be made aware of opportunities and provided the tools and guidance to seize them.

Too often entities and institutions just do bare minimum to publicize opportunities in tech careers to the broader population. There is not enough publicity around what is needed to fulfill these types of positions and how one can go about obtaining a role after they have qualified themselves. A key question is how to ensure that a larger segment of diverse communities is taking advantage of opportunities in the tech sector.

One area of proven success in terms of marketing careers and professionals to diverse populations is that of athletes and entertainers. The genesis of the motivation for individuals to aspire to fulfill these roles is the mass marketing of them on different media platforms.

The contracts, lifestyles, and daily movements of athletes and entertainers are chronicled vociferously by many major media outlets. This kind of promotion is also necessary for people to eventually be motivated to pursue other career fields in large numbers. Strategic marketing techniques can be directed to populations of people who need to be inundated with alternatives and empowered by options that can lead to a better way of life. Marketing has proven to be effective and should be incorporated to provide consistent exposure to emerging opportunities in the tech sector.

Exposure to opportunities can be further disseminated by incorporating voter registration and "get out the vote" type strategies for increased tech career awareness. Voter registration and turnout efforts are often proactive, targeted, and intentional. Organizers frequently don't just say that "the election will be on a certain day, now register and vote." They make aggressive efforts to bring voter registration forms to where people live and gather for an extended period. Mobilization efforts like "Souls to the Polls" and transportation options are provided to get people to be eligible and take the necessary steps to vote.

Candidates put signs and advertisements across various communities to bring awareness of their platform and to encourage people to vote. The same kind of direct and intentional targeting can be employed to get students to buy into and take the necessary steps to take advantage of emerging tech opportunities.

Ultimately, exposure to different career fields only works if students are equipped with the competencies to be able to fulfill the roles. There is a need to key in on math because to successfully obtain a degree in most tech majors, math is the key to opening a gate that has locked far too many students out. Too many students don't even have the option of majoring in one of the emerging tech fields because they don't have the math competency to complete the coursework.

Supremely talented math teachers are the key to producing competent math students who will be able to pass the requisite coursework to complete degrees in tech fields. There is a need to identify the best math teaching talent and incentivize them to come to and/or stay in the education profession. This will likely require doubling or tripling the average pay of a classroom teacher to have salaries that are competitive enough to recruit top tier talent.

An intensive focus on strategies to support students who may be behind in math competency when they reach post-secondary education institutions is also needed. Most people don't necessarily have an advanced innate ability to do math; they just have to recognize the importance of it and be motivated to do it.

In an era of significant student disengagement with the explosion of virtual learning platforms during the Covid-19 pandemic, it is also a worthy endeavor to take a deeper look at areas where engagement is high. One such area is Amateur Athletic Union (AAU) and travel basketball teams.

AAU and travel basketball has been a vehicle for many young people to travel to different parts of the country, connect with other student-athletes from diverse socioeconomic backgrounds, and test their skills against their local area and the nation's best players. Similar structures should be put in place for aspiring tech students and professionals. The space to be able to compete and put one's skills up against the best in their community, state, and nation would be incredible in terms of being able to raise interest and receive recognition for one's efforts.

The same kind of hype, passion, and enthusiasm that AAU basketball produces can be generated if parallel systems for tech were put in place. A parallel system would include making the competition public, sponsoring travel, and creating an environment similar to big time AAU events with college recruiters present and scholarships on the line. The creation of multiple summer tournaments and high-profile events may help to shift some of the tremendous athletic momentum that is prevalent in many communities into tech. This type of momentum can produce the drive to go after tech dreams.

After the dream is ignited in people, efforts must continue to integrate historically underrepresented communities into the new economy. It is one task to construct career pathways in the tech sector; it is another to inspire and motivate people to take the necessary steps to take advantage of these pathways. Each of these formidable tasks will require dedicated and intentional efforts. Completing one without the other will not bring the transformative impact that is needed for genuine inclusion and an equity of opportunity. Tech dreams can be used to accelerate people's ability and drive to plug into the opportunities, pathways, and programs that are being created by educational institutions and other entities.

Inspiring Tech Discipline

I wrote previously about the need to inspire "tech dreams." Dreams need to be ignited for students to have the internal motivation to want to pursue careers in the emerging tech sector. This, however, is just one needed component on the road to the actualization of the dream. Every dream requires discipline to bring it to fruition. Motivation will help students get started, but discipline will keep them progressing towards the fulfillment of their promise.

Discipline will be the bridge that students can use to get from dreaming their desire to accomplishing it. The discipline that is required to persist on the road to completing the qualifications to be equipped to adequately fulfill a gainfully compensated role in the tech industry often involves the ability to delay gratification, put forth consistent effort, and embrace the developmental process.

One example of the implementation of discipline is the journey of my younger brother, Marlon Bright, in obtaining a bachelor's degree in computer engineering at Florida International University (FIU). I have listed four takeaways from his journey that can be used to inspire "tech discipline" in others:

1. Put in Overtime

Marlon joined the FIU men's basketball team as a walk-on and eventually worked his way into playing significant minutes and being a meaningful contributor to the team. Playing Division I college basketball requires a tremendous amount of time that includes training, practicing, games, travel, film study, and other associated activities. When you combine that with a rigorous computer engineering course schedule, time becomes a big factor. In order for Marlon to maintain his close to 4.0 grade point average (GPA), he had to put in a lot of "overtime".

Overtime consisted of study sessions in the engineering lab after games that frequently lasted until well after midnight. It also meant studying on airplanes and buses, in hotels, and various other settings to keep up with his coursework and learning workload. One key that kept him engaged for several hours at a time was that he found areas of interest that were connected to the areas that he was studying. For example, if he was working on a project to build a customer management application, he would look at it as if he were building a game. He found ways to connect math to how airplanes, rockets, and satellites worked.

New perspectives can help students see that a particularly hard concept can help them to understand how a computer or game console works. Putting in "overtime" can be an enjoyable experience when it is connected to a passion and a purpose.

2. Make Key Tradeoffs

A cost is what you give up for something else. There are tradeoffs that must be made to accomplish certain things. Marlon chose to make some key tradeoffs at pivotal points to complete his computer engineering degree. He grew up playing sports and enjoyed his first two years of playing on the FIU basketball team, but as the coursework in his major got more difficult it became harder to navigate around the significant number of classes that he had to miss for games and travel. He decided to not play basketball during his third year at FIU and redirect that time into his studies and other extra-curricular activities on campus.

A key to him having the flexibility to make this tradeoff was that he went to school on an academic scholarship as opposed to an athletic scholarship. He made a cost-benefit estimation that having a great year of basketball was not worth sacrificing the academic learning that he needed to get from his computer engineering curriculum to set him up for his long-term future. Students need to ask themselves if certain activities are worth the cost. They must do their own cost-benefit analysis and be able to make key tradeoffs.

One of the additional endeavors that he took on while sitting out of basketball during that season was to work on a research project with a professor in the computer science department. He volunteered to do additional work to obtain some research experience with the hope that it would bolster his graduate school applications. The professor happened to be connected to a partnership with IBM that sponsored students to do international research. Marlon was selected to be a part of that project and garnered a paid internship with the Barcelona Supercomputing Center in Spain. He ended up being at the right place at the right time, but it was "tech discipline" that put him in the right place to be selected. His tradeoff paid off.

3.   Be Aggressive About Getting the Help that You Need

A part of having "tech discipline" is doing all that you can in pursuit of an objective and then going and getting the help that you need to do the things that you can't initially do. You must do your homework as well as you can do it, but you also have to be aggressive about tapping into the resources that you have to learn things.

Marlon sought help with problems during his professor's office hours, he joined student study groups, and utilized online resources to get the assistance that he needed to maintain a stellar GPA and ensure that he was learning the necessary concepts that he needed to progress in his program. Institutions of higher education typically have a great deal of resources to assist students with their learning and academic development. Many of these services are underutilized by the students who need them the most.

Collaborating with likeminded students can offer great benefits like exploring new ways to look at concepts, learning new study skills, and holding each other accountable. A student that has a clear understanding of the material can sometimes explain it to his or her peers with more clarity than even the professor can. If students want a clearer understanding of aspects of coursework that they may be struggling with, then they must be diligent about seeking out the help that they need.

4. Expand Your Horizons

The tech sector can seem like a different world with a different language. There is a unique set of tools and experiences that people need to be able to operate in that world. Accessing that world at a high level requires one to expand their horizons. It requires having a desire to pursue and create experiences and will take a person to the next level. Discipline is a pre-requisite for the development of needed skills and to be in position to experience certain opportunities.

Marlon's hard work to keep his G.P.A. at an elite level put him in a position to be eligible for great summer internship opportunities like the Goldman Sachs Technology Division, the Barcelona Supercomputing Center, and the Southwest Research Institute that he was able to participate in. His grades were a great start, but they would likely not have been sufficient if not accompanied by other efforts like utilizing campus resources, taking on leadership positions in student organizations, and participating in extra-curricular activities.

For example, in preparation for an internship fair that eventually led to his summer role with Goldman Sachs, he took advantage of the resources that FIU offered. He went to the career center and utilized support for resume assistance and mock interviews. He took the time to research the companies that would be at the fair in advance and applied to positions that he desired in advance. The discipline to put in this additional work paid dividends when the fair took place. He set himself up for success.

He was also very specific about what he wanted to do so that he could pursue and create opportunities that would push him in the right direction. As he continued to go in his desired direction with discipline, his desires began to manifest one after another. Marlon went on to get a master's degree in aerospace engineering from the University of Texas. He currently works for John Deere as a Tech Stack Systems Architect where he drives advancements in technology application to agricultural crop production globally using technologies such as machine learning, artificial intelligence, and cloud computing.

His work has taken him all over the world to destinations that include Australia, Brazil, India, China, Germany, France, and the United Kingdom. He was focused on what he wanted to do, he enjoyed the process, and he remained persistent until he accomplished his desired goals. One can't accomplish the tech dream without going through the tech process.

It can feel to some who are pursuing tech careers like they are trying to break into an inaccessible world. Shifting a limiting mindset and belief system is the first step to being able to access the abundant opportunities that are available in the "tech world", but discipline is the admission ticket that students will ultimately have to punch to complete their journey to fulfilling their tech dreams.

Inspiring Tech Bridges

I wrote in the sections that preceded this one about the need to inspire tech dreams and discipline in students for them to be able to qualify themselves for roles in the emerging tech sector. There is also a need to inspire tech bridges to be constructed or reinforced for adult learners to have pathways to cross over into positions in tech fields that can improve their quality of life and deploy their talents in different ways. I have listed three strategies that tech bridge builders can use in their quest to find ways to connect adult learners to programs at higher education institutions that can equip them for accelerating opportunities in the tech sector.

1.   Adapt to the needs of adult learners and go where they are.

It is obvious that working adults typically have a different set of perspectives and responsibilities than their counterparts who may be coming directly from high school. Adapting course scheduling and delivery to fit their needs will be a critical component of building the bridges that are needed for people to cross from one career path to another.

There is also a need to identify where potential adult students congregate in order to get information to them about opportunities in the tech sector. This allows for the broad dissemination of information and gives room for additional relationship building that comes with the follow up questions and answer sessions where interested potential students can garner further insights into how they can make the transition into a tech career.

Trade organizations and unions can also be great partners in upskilling their members with additional technology-related tools that they can apply to their current career paths. Parents of existing students who recently matriculated from high school are also a group that can be engaged through orientations and other communication forums where they can receive knowledge that can lead to the upliftment of their circumstances. If they can be shown a path for how they can get it done, then all that is needed is the belief that they have the ability to do it and the inspiration to take the necessary steps to complete it.

2. Lead with emerging opportunities and compensation potential.

A bridge into tech careers alone will not be sufficient if people don't believe that the cost that they will have to pay to cross the bridge is worth it. Finding and keeping relevant motivation is paramount. The gas tank of motivation is one that must be refilled frequently. Finding different ways to provide students with reminders of how their hard work and sacrifice can pay off will bring long term benefits in the areas of retention and completion.

The potential salaries that people can make both starting off and as they progress in their new career field should be presented to potential students along with examples of adult learners who have successfully transitioned from other fields into tech. This helps to strengthen the belief that it can happen for them as well. Additionally, those who have already made the transition into tech positions can also serve as mentors for others who aspire to. The cultivation of mentorship programs can be a "win-win" for everyone involved if structured appropriately. Mentorship is needed at all levels of life.

Emerging opportunities in tech are a big part of where the

future of the economy is headed. This case should be made to adult learners that they can prepare and position themselves now to have skills that will become increasingly more relevant. College and university support staff can help students to identify and fill their skill gaps and explain how the programming can provide a personalized and skill-based education that can help them to fulfill their career promise and purpose.

3. Clearly lay out the path.

People can run faster and more confidently when they know where they are going. Clearly laying out the path over the bridge can alleviate a lot of doubt, fear, and worry and allow those energies to be directed in a more positive and productive direction. Clarity and confidence are two keys to retaining students once they have entered a given program.

Clearly laying out the path for adult learners involves identifying vivid descriptions of programing and utilizing appropriate media options that are consistent with the intended communication objectives to optimize message delivery and the processing of the message. Various forms of communication with students and prospective students can be considered and evaluated on an ongoing basis as potential delivery channels for communication including the website which is typically the number one source of advertising for programs. Websites should be bold, exciting, highly informative, and easy to navigate.

The path for students may be to reskill, upskill, or fully transition to a different career. Any of these routes can be laid out with clarity so that students can understand and buy into completing their journey in the program.

Additionally, the specific skill sets and core competencies that they would acquire in a given program should be explained. These sets of skills operate like currency in the tech world. It is important to explain the transferrable nature of these competencies and how they can be applied across various job categories in multiple sectors. Doing this can increase the motivation to become competent in these areas because of the versatile way that they can be applied. This provides the people who obtain a level of competency with more options for deploying their knowledge, skills, and abilities.

Higher education institutions can play a key role in constructing bridges that inspire adult learners to repurpose themselves, reconnect to their dreams, and generate new aspirations. The poet Langston Hughes wrote "hold fast to dreams, for if dreams die, life is a broken-winged bird, that cannot fly." As the years go by, some adult learners may have abandoned some of the dreams that they once had. They may have buried their dreams, but the economy of the future provides a way for people to go dig up dreams that they once had and connect to them in a new way.

There are those who may feel trapped in what they feel is a "dead end" job and have surrendered to a limited projection of what they can be. Ultimately, inspiring the building of tech bridges requires bridge builders at educational institutions, workforce development organizations, and corporate entities to find innovative ways to construct pathways for adult learners to equip themselves to improve the quality of their lives by crossing over into tech-oriented careers.

Inspiring Tech Pipelines

There is no doubt that the development of ways to disrupt the school-to-prison pipeline has been a priority in discussions and initiatives at multiple levels of the criminal justice and educational systems. There have been advancements like the growth of diversion programs that give youth a second chance, mentorship initiatives, and some relaxation of certain draconian drug laws.

For the persistent patterns that have led to what has been framed as the "school-to-prison pipeline" to be abated; very strong alternatives must continue to be developed, fortified, and supported. One strong alternative pipeline is in the area of computer science. It has great potential to redirect youth into an area of great economic viability and the potential for impactful social innovation.

One strategy is to build upon existing assessments that measure computational thinking and identify students as early as middle school who have advanced abilities in these areas. According to research from the International Journal of Child-Computer Interaction "there are large differences in computational ability among middle school students even before they start to learn coding" (Román-González et al., 2018).

The article posited that "computational thinking (CT) is arising as a set of problem-solving skills that must be acquired by the new generations of students to fully understand and participate in our computer-based world." Students who have been identified by these assessments with high levels of computational talent can be put on an accelerated pathway that includes a dedicated coding curriculum, robotics competitions, industry specific instruction, tech-sector mentorship, and other developmental activities.

Many communities have done a great job of identifying those with athletic talent at an early age and creating many camps, activities, and infrastructures that produce environments for their ability to flourish. Players are often pushed to the edge of their ability by members of the community, parents, coaches, peers, and teammates. The standard excellence that is produced by the cumulative expectations from these groups has generated generations of exceptional athletes and teams in the face of significant economic odds in many cases.

Stereotypes also play a role in what route students pursue and the level of energy, effort, and identity that they invest in their pursuit. The term stereotype, which the Merriam-Webster Dictionary defines as "something conforming to a fixed or general pattern especially: a standardized mental picture that is held in common by members of a group and that represents an oversimplified opinion, prejudiced attitude, or uncritical judgment" ("Stereotype," n.d.), often carries a negative connotation with it. A stereotype can take on a different level of impact when it is believed and internalized by the person that it is projected on.

The level of one's internal investment in a stereotype that is projected on them from the outside can impact how much they adjust their decision-making and actions to fulfill the stereotype in some way. The power of a stereotype lies in how much it is believed by those who are projecting it and by those who are on the receiving end of it.

I contend that there are circumstances where stereotypes can cause people to raise their level of performance in a certain area because of their desire to fulfill it. For example, if one is expected to be an athlete or participate in a certain sport or sports based on societal stereotypes, then this could result in a range of consequences depending on the influences that one is exposed to. Research from Denis Dumas and Kevin Dunbar on what they describe as "The Creative Stereotype Effect" found that stereotypes related to creativity can both enhance and diminish individuals' performance" and that "stereotypes can also produce better performance if the individual believes their group should or will perform well on a given task" (Dumas & Dunbar, 2016)

The athletic stereotype is put on many people, and it may help them to perform at a higher level because they rise to meet that expectation and there can be an extra sense of confidence as if they are doing something that they were designed to do. There can be an enhanced level of fluidity in how they perform. A confidence that emerges from the subconscious and supports athletic achievement at a high level.

Similar methods can be employed to build new pipelines to computer science and other tech sector careers. The level of individual and community beliefs about certain narratives is a key component to how related patterns of behavior can become institutionalized. Both communities and the media can choose whatever it wants to make important. They can choose whoever they deem as being valuable and give them an elevated status.

Through highlighting and uplifting those who have excelled in tech sector careers, communities can develop and nurture the required confidence, knowledge, and skills to excel in tech pipelines. Athletes from a particular area who make it into the professional ranks often become symbols for many others who hope to follow in their footsteps.

An example of a superstar in the tech field that should be a household name for people is Randy Raymond. Raymond should be highlighted not just because he excelled at Suncoast High School in West Palm Beach, FL, graduated from Harvard University with a degree in computer science, or is a software engineer. Those accomplishments are among the things that make him successful, but what makes him especially significant is that he has led the charge to establish a new cohort of the Google Computer Science Summer Institute in Florida. Raymond attended the institute after his senior year in high school and it was a transformative experience for him that helped to shape his future career path.

His desire and efforts towards blazing new pathways for students coming behind him to have access to the same kind of opportunities that he had should be celebrated. The cultivation and fortification of supported pathways into tech fields like computer science and the mass marketing of examples of excellence like Raymond are both key to building new pipelines to prosperity that can serve as powerful alternatives to the destructive school-to-prison pipeline. We need an acceleration of intentional efforts to utilize the power of positive stereotypes, produce more pipelines into tech fields, and heavily promote role models in these areas.

Inspiring Tech Economics

One could argue that in many areas across the country where the tech sector is exploding that it is an economic imperative for more people to participate in the lucrative career opportunities that are within the space. For populations that have been historically excluded from many wealth building opportunities even more is at stake as inflation and the rapidly accelerating costs of living increase financial pressure.

For various reasons, people of color have been consistently overrepresented in the low wage labor market including bias, discrimination, deficits in social capital, and lack of access to equitable educational opportunities.

There is little doubt that money is a significant factor in why people may pursue careers in tech and why it is quickly becoming an economic imperative for those who have the desire and discipline to qualify themselves for prosperity in the space to be provided opportunities. Fields like engineering, computer science, and the like earn anywhere from 20% to 85% more than the average salary depending on what state people are located according to data compiled by business.org (Wheelwright, 2021).

The focus on earned wages is more pronounced for populations that have been historically excluded from many wealth building opportunities because they are more often faced with having to purchase major assets like homes with their own income versus those who are able to make these kinds of acquisitions with significant assistance from wealth that has been funneled down to them from previous generations.

A recent article in Bloomberg highlighted the growing number of people who are getting down payments or in some cases entire houses financed from parents. "Parents are increasingly helping their adult children purchase homes, whether that means co-signing a mortgage, giving money for a down payment or buying the property outright, according to real estate agents across the country" per their reporting (Ballentine & Cachero, 2022).

These are the kinds of wealth transfers that propel a person far beyond what they earn on their jobs. These transfers are often hidden as the Bloomberg piece alludes to in stating that "it's hard to determine exactly how many buyers are receiving help from their parents, in part because few are willing to discuss how they're paying for a new home."

Without the advantage of in-life wealth transfers that can subsidize college costs, cars, private school payments, credit card payments, medical bills, business start-up money, housing, and other significant purchases; increased integration into the tech sector and other higher income industries becomes even more important.

A shift from being underrepresented to overrepresented in higher paying career fields can be a game changer as it pertains to the economic development of historically marginalized communities. This shift can happen by identifying the undervalued assets in these communities beginning with those who have the ability to excel in tech sector careers but may not know it or have the proper systems and supports in place to bring it to fruition.

An inflection point is imminent in several metro areas like Miami, Austin, Nashville, and Orlando. Rents in Miami, for example, went up almost 41% from April 2021 to April 2022 according to Corelogic. Principal economist at Corelogic, Molly Boesel, was quoted in a Bloomberg article saying that "we expect single-family rent growth to continue to increase at a rapid pace throughout 2022" (Tanzi, 2022, para. 3). Cities that used to be affordable for the middle and working classes may only be in reach for very high-income earners or those who are able to make purchases with wealth that has been passed down from previous generations. There is a rapidly closing window for people who are outside of those two categories or don't already own housing in certain areas to be able to secure it on their own.

For these reasons and more, infrastructures of opportunity that provide supported pathways for people to gain the credentials and social capital to successfully integrate into gainful tech sector employment should be a key economic development strategy.

Inspiring Tech Participation

The first step to winning a game is to be a participant in it. The consequences of a continued under-participation in tech careers by historically marginalized populations will lead to a furthering of economic stratification and inequity. More avenues for participation must be developed and more people must participate for collective economic empowerment at the community level to take place.

This is the time to find innovative ways to get students of all ages off the sidelines and into the game. Too many people are watching from the sidelines believing that they don't have what it takes to be able to get out on the field. Limiting beliefs may prevent some from participating when they have the potential and capacity to flourish.

Sometimes it just takes a spark, like an interest in building and designing things that can provide the motivation to move forward on taking additional steps like learning programming development platforms such as Python and Javascript.

There is a need for initial exposure to the multitude of roles within the tech economy and then for pathways to be created for interested students to delve deeper into their preferred area of interest. This will take both competent people and dedicated resources to provide some level of consistency and continuity.

It is important to note that everyone does not have to be directly involved in software development. There are various ways to participate in tech-related programming including robotics, gaming, graphic design, sales, and marketing among others. There are also transferrable skills that may have been cultivated in other industries that can be utilized within the universe of tech economy participation.

Getting people started and participating at some level puts them in a position where they can build momentum and gain skills that can qualify them to play at a higher level. Capacity can be increased after participation has begun. There will no doubt be gaps in the ability of people to play initially, but if they are given equitable facilities, instruction, and opportunities then their chances to be competitive in the tech marketplace are likely to increase dramatically.

Capacity building activities can also be embedded into the co-curricular and extra-curricular culture and processes of schools and communities in the same way that sports like basketball and football are. In sports, player capacity and performance are improved through coaching and practice. Skills are sharpened through camps, drills, and competitions.

Additionally, there are individual regimens and ways that people can work on their craft outside of formal settings. These are all ways that sports training methods can be transferred to tech. Apprenticeships, certificate programs, and other training platforms can also be established or bolstered to get unskilled or semi-skilled individuals the additional training that they need to be competitive in the tech workplace.

Critical tech courses can also be embedded in the core curriculum of school systems. The relevance of some existing required classes is questionable at best. A "Flintstones" academic program is not optimal for a "Jetsons" world. Development opportunities that provide exposure, information, hands-on activities, and connectivity to further capacity building infrastructures are starting points where people can identify their interests and accelerate in their chosen pathways.

After the initiation of participation and capacity building, there must be intentional efforts to open up the doors of tech employment and entrepreneurship. Exposure and opportunity without tangible benefits at the culmination of the process is not sufficient. Preparing people to walk through the gates of tech opportunity will be to little avail if the gates are locked. Beating down the doors with qualified applicants is the first step to nullifying the excuse of not finding enough "qualified" tech workers.

Economic development for most people means gaining access to a higher paying job, the window is open with tech for more individuals to do that and ultimately improve financial conditions for themselves, their families, and their communities.

A radical change in tech participation that is initiated and sustained would go a long way towards producing the kind of economic transformation that can lift individuals and communities into higher levels of educational achievement, social mobility, and better health outcomes.

Inspiring Tech On-Ramps

When it comes to inspiring the development of more on-ramps into tech for youth, beginning in areas where many students already spend a lot of their free time is a good place to start and expand. I contend that more on-ramps, defined by the Merriam-Webster Dictionary as "a ramp by which one enters a limited-access highway", are needed to get more people into a tech sector that can be reasonably described as a limited-access highway to those who are not already in it, have had little exposure to it, or lack access to high levels of training related to it.

There is a need to find ways to meet students where they are and integrate meaningful content and curriculum into what they are doing. This is key to drumming up enough of what it takes to attract and retain those who may not have otherwise had an initial inclination or interest.

Even with access to some form of computer science education for example, there still needs to be a great deal of promotion and on-ramps built for students to be motivated to enroll and persist through completion. Packaging opportunities for tech skill attainment in a format that many already enjoy like gaming is one way of building tech on-ramps.

Gaming is a hugely popular area among teens and young adults and is where many voluntarily spend a great deal of their discretionary time. It is a multi-billion-dollar industry with career opportunities not only in actual game playing, but also in game development, illustration, legal, marketing, and sports medicine. Esports is an area that can be leveraged to fuel new opportunities for entrepreneurship and be a gateway for young people to explore a variety of Science, Technology, Engineering, and Mathematics (STEM) fields.

More traditional sports like basketball, football, and baseball can also be a vehicle and platform to deliver tech education and increase tech competency. The utility of tech competency keeps going even after a student-athlete's ability or eligibility to play a particular sport runs out. Leveraging the power of sports to build new tech on-ramps can get people on highways that will help them develop valuable competencies and skills that pay the bills.

One key to transferring the momentum that sports can generate into tech is through the infusion of the marketing, promotion, and social status that are currently utilized in popular sports. This involves the reinforcement of images of people who have successfully made it into careers in the tech sector. Consistent exposure to these individuals and having discussions about their journeys can increase the level of belief that others can also ascend to similar stations through their own unique pathways.

Finding ways to elevate the social status of those students who are performing well in different areas of tech competency to a level that is on par with star athletes would also go a long way towards getting more people on the tech highway. The gratification that is attached to family, community, and social celebration is one of many motivating factors that can drive sustained elite athletic performance.

Another key is the insertion of healthy levels of pressurized competition. The best high school and college athletes have often developed their ability over thousands of hours of pressurized competition over many years. The adage that "iron sharpens iron" applies here. Athletic competition often prompts players to spend extra hours working on their craft, strategize with teammates to improve their performance, receive dedicated instruction and encouragement from coaches who have a vested interest in their success, figure out how to solve complex problems, and perform under the pressure of enthusiastic audiences. On-ramps that incorporate these elements can also be infused into tech programming.

Additionally, building on existing curriculum bases or helping teachers to establish new ones is a way to keep students on the tech highway after they have accessed it via an on-ramp. The development of new on-ramps can be accompanied by the building of additional supports and partnerships around existing programming in a way that complements what is already in place. For example, tech sector professionals can be incorporated into lessons and development strategies for teachers, field trips to tech companies can be facilitated, and further exposure to the world of work through internship and job opportunities can be made available.

After spending years on the ground in different communities and seeing the need to an increased level of exposure and connectivity to opportunities as well as the elevation of policy issues related to socioeconomic mobility, I launched the National Brighter Ways Forward Initiative in December 2022 with the aim of inspiring the creation of more on-ramps into careers and economic opportunity in the tech sector among other fields. It will consist of events and programming across the country that will have three objectives:

1. exposure to career and economic opportunities for students and families,

2. connectivity to longer-term training and development opportunities, and

3. the elevation of broader policy issues that are of relevance to socioeconomic mobility in each area.

The goal is to help create a climate that inspires the building of more on-ramps onto avenues of prosperity across the country. This would be a game changer for the economic well-being and the holistic upliftment of communities.

Inspiring Tech Context

It would likely not make sense for someone to repeatedly run sprints, do agility drills, and hoist their body into another person for no reason. It isn't until the context of football and the opportunities that participation in the sport entails that it would make sense for those students who choose to play to engage in it.

The context around football has been infused with value. There are clear models of success, scholarship opportunities to major universities, lucrative professional contracts, elevated social status, and the potential to dramatically change the economic conditions for themselves and their families in place. These are all aspects that add to the context around the motivation for participation in the sport.

The context of sports and entertainment stardom can inspire extreme levels of practice, perseverance, and production on playing courts and fields. Context addresses the important "for what" question.

The meaning that context provides can make a critical difference in tech educational curriculum like computer science. Coding programs like Python, JavaScript, or even critical subjects like Algebra are much less likely to have relevance to students if there is not a value infused context attached to them.

Exposure to people who are operating at high levels of tech, their lifestyles, and their workplaces is critical to providing context to the content that students are learning. This context gives relevance to curriculum and study that may otherwise seem disconnected.

I believe that there is a need to intentionally build context around computer science education specifically. The utility of tech skillsets like competence in computer programming languages is multidimensional as it is used to build websites and software applications that operate cellphones, thermostats, airplanes, elevators, video games, social media, and so much more. These items were all brought to us in large part by computer scientists and engineers. This is all a part of tech context. Pretty much everything runs on software nowadays.

Reinforcing the utility and versality of educational content and where you can take it is a vital part of inspiring tech context. One of the dictionary.com definitions of context is "the set of circumstances or facts that surround a particular event, situation, etc." The context of why accelerating in tech education generally and computer science more specifically in South Florida, for example, where I am based is key.

There is an economic imperative here that accompanies the need to inspire tech context. This context includes understanding the industry standards and skillsets that will have an elevated level of marketplace demand and value for current students as they transition into the workforce in a South Florida that leads the nation in the growth of rent and housing prices and is among the perennial leaders in economic inequality.

Employer partners can be critical allies in inspiring tech context because they can provide real-time relevance to curriculum and insight into the different dimensions and ways that it can be applied. These partners are also critical because all industries, including tech, are constantly evolving and the preparation process for tech career pathways should constantly be retooled and updated to reflect the latest changes in economic conditions and in-demand skillsets.

Inspiring tech context requires going beyond the content and the classroom. It entails building infrastructures of opportunity that complement the curriculum, providing exposure that brings life to the content, and finding ways to dramatize the socioeconomic imperative of bringing individuals and communities into alignment with what is and will be a pivotal part of the economy.

How Colleges and Universities Can Be Blockchain Technology Community Hubs

The rapid advancement of blockchain technology and cryptocurrency has made it imperative for the higher education community to adapt and respond to this economic phenomenon. There is great opportunity for colleges and universities to expand their economic impact and footprint through the proliferation of information, exposure, and opportunities for people to create a better financial future for themselves and their families.

There is a tremendous need for greater education on how the permissionless nature of blockchain technology can have the power to break through existing barriers in the economic system like lack of access to credit and capital that has often thwarted prosperity for underserved and historically marginalized communities.

Financial institutions have traditionally been gatekeepers

for lending, borrowing, trading, investing, and other similar activities. The historical patterns of behavior by many of these gatekeepers have had a disproportionately discriminatory impact of a significant number of people who have found themselves locked out of avenues of wealth building. Blockchain eliminates the need for unnecessary third, fourth, and fifth parties when accessing the services listed above and avoids some of the friction that has permeated these processes.

Instead of speaking to a person to try to get a loan or relying on a bank to complete a transaction, a user can interact with a smart contract that is governed by an algorithm that is responsible for granting its users' loans and facilitating transactions. The only requirements for individuals to get involved are a smart device, internet connection, and the deposit of the capital required to fulfill the collateralization ratios that are set by the algorithm or set of rules that govern a software application.

In similar fashion to how the internet improves conditions for how information is shared globally, blockchain enables additional functionality through immutable data transfer. This means that users of blockchain can send valuable data to another person without having to worry about intervention or tampering by a third party.

Colleges and universities can lead the conversation around how the internet has changed the way that the world cooperates and how blockchain technology is a response to the failures of current internet infrastructure, regulation, and global monetary policy.

Recognizing the history of the internet and its roots in the most prominent universities around the world, educational institutions are best positioned to be at the helm of the changes taking place as the internet progresses into its most promising iterations, Web 3.0. As the leaders of research and educational initiatives in society's most fruitful communities, colleges and universities are primed to be opportunity hubs for communities to be empowered through this significant global development.

It is imperative for plans of action to be developed to take advantage of the financial inclusivity and prosperity that blockchain technology can provide for otherwise underserved and underprivileged communities. Institutions of higher education can be the conveners that community partners, faith leaders, elected officials, and others can organize with to increase economic equity in the emerging fintech (finance and technology) sector.

Why Access to Computer Science Education Should Be the New Space Race

President John F. Kennedy in a 1962 speech at Rice University spoke about why the country should have the goal of going to the moon by saying that "we choose to go to the moon in this decade and do the other things, not because they are easy, but because they are hard, because that goal will serve to organize and measure the best of our energies and skills, because that challenge is one that we are willing to accept, one we are unwilling to postpone, and one which we intend to win, and the others, too" (Kennedy, 1962).

As it was in 1962 with space, it is now with technology in general and computer science specifically. The consequences of not making computer science education a national priority are dire. The next generation could be left without a core competency that will be needed to be a central part of the economy of the future not because they lack the talent but because they lack the access. Immediate and urgent action is required.

Expanding access to computer science at an accelerated rate in 2022 is pivotal. Computer science courses in high school should be the norm as opposed to an anomaly. The need to expand access to computer science and the broader push for the integration of more people into the emerging tech fields is becoming more urgent as the cost-of-living surges. Equipping more people to have the opportunity to be a part of the economic mainstream that is represented by burgeoning tech ecosystems is paramount.

Randy Raymond, a Google software engineer is on a mission to help expand access to computer science in the emerging tech hotbed of South Florida. Raymond knows from his own life experience what kind of impact early exposure to computer science can have on the trajectory of people's lives. His first exposure to tech was through making video games at 10 years old through software called RPG Maker for the computer. He had to learn how to code to make the game.

Raymond never got any formal training in the field until he took Advanced Placement (AP) Computer Science in his senior year of high school at Suncoast Community High School in West Palm Beach, Florida where they also had a computer science track.

A recent article in Diverse: Issues in Higher Education about AP Computer Science highlighted a study that showed "that students who took AP CSP were over three times as likely to major in computer science when they advanced to college. They are also twice as likely to enroll for AP CSA, a course that focuses on programming languages. Those increases were seen across all desired demographics, including first generation college students" (Herder, 2021)

Raymond then attended the Google Computer Science Summer Institute (CSSI) after his senior year in high school. This experience solidified his decision to major in Computer Science at Harvard University. CSSI "is a three-week introduction to computer science for graduating high school seniors with a passion for technology- especially students from historically underrepresented groups in the field..... It's an intensive, interactive, hands-on and fun program that seeks to inspire the tech leaders and innovators of tomorrow by supporting the study of computer science, software engineering and other closely related subjects."

The extension and portability of programs like the Google CSSI are vital at this time. Raymond desires to give students the opportunity to see the passion that they can find in technology through partnering with public and private entities to make these kinds of programs more accessible.

The current practice of companies paying exorbitant amounts of money to sponsor international talent through H-1B visa and other mechanisms can be redirected towards the development of new pipelines from communities that currently lack access. Corporations should be incentivized to invest in underserved communities through the creation of accelerated pathways in computer science.

The K-12 and higher educational system should build partnerships with these corporations and others to expose students to STEM careers and curriculum early in the education process. Higher education institutions can partner with school districts and/or community organizations to expand access in the short term until more permanent computer science courses are embedded for the masses of students. This can be done initially through existing avenues like AP Computer Science and dual enrollment arrangements.

Like Kennedy's "Space Race", this new push for access to computer science education will take a massive commitment of money for equipment and financial investment in people to pay talented instructors and facilitators competitive salaries to execute the mission. This public policy commitment and national priority placement is needed in order for people to be prepared to take advantage of the plethora of opportunities that the tech sector has to offer.

Grassroots Push for Computer Science Education Gears Up

For close to a year, I strategized and worked with Randy Raymond, a software engineer at Google, to continue the push to make access to computer science education the new "Space Race" and create models that schools can scale to deliver instruction to students. We believe that this movement can be expanded and go a long way towards increasing diversity in fields like engineering and computing.

We have visited schools in South Florida and met with administrators, teachers, and students to assess current levels of computer science access and instruction and to find ways to add value to present academic programming. We sought to combine Randy's knowledge of computer science from an academic perspective and its practical application in the economy with my experience facilitating many partnerships between K-12 schools, higher education institutions, corporations, and non-profit entities.

Randy had early access to a computational thinking assessment that has been shown to have a significant level of predictive ability as it pertains to identifying students who are naturally inclined to perform well in computer-science oriented activities. We drew parallels between the assessment and the way that young basketball and football players are evaluated at early ages and put into infrastructures and systems where their talent can be nurtured and developed.

We wanted to create a parallel system of development for computer science and other fields. The aim is not to segregate those who score well on the assessment to the exclusion of others but rather to bring more students into an advanced level of exposure and training in addition to those who were already interested in the space and wanted to pursue computer science and other tech related areas.

In the systems that we are endeavoring to create, everyone has an opportunity to play just like in basketball for example. Some people play pick-up basketball, some play in intramural games, some play on the freshman team, some play on the junior varsity team, some play on the varsity team, some are starters for the varsity team, some also play for an Amateur Athletic Union (AAU) team, some play AAU on one of the top circuits like Nike EYBL, some play in top EYBL tournaments like the Peach Jam.

We will begin piloting the initial stage of this concept at a South Florida area middle school during the Spring 2023 semester. The school has an existing science, technology, engineering, and mathematics (S.T.E.M.) magnet program where half of the students in the pilot will come from. The other half will come from the general student population.

All of the students will take the aforementioned Computational Thinking Assessment which will help to inform what version of a computer science curriculum they will receive. The curriculum will be personalized to each student based on their ability level which will be approximated based on the assessment. Some students will receive the Google Computer Science (CS) First curriculum that uses the Scratch block-based coding language to introduce computer science. Those who score particularly well on the assessment will be introduced to computer science through a JavaScript based curriculum.

We will work together with community partners to provide an assortment of career readiness and life skills workshops for the cohort, facilitate field trips aimed at exposure to the world of work, and bring in different tech sector mentors to provide guidance and inspiration to students.

This grassroots push in South Florida to create more avenues for people to become software programmers and elevate the importance of students having access to high quality computer science education is set to gear up in 2023. The time to start where you are with what you have is now.

PART 3: SOCIOECONOMIC MOBILITY: EDUCATION, CAREER, AND ECONOMICS

Part three deals with socioeconomic mobility more broadly. This section is divided into three dimensions of mobility: education, career, and economics. Mobility refers to the ability to move between different levels of poverty. It entails progress in this context in the areas of economics, education, and career trajectory. The commentary and reflections that follow cover a broad range of the ramifications of multiple factors related to all three aspects of socioeconomic mobility that are targeted in this section.

Economic Mobility

Broken Dreams and Financial Illusions: The Secret Depression of Black Men

There is a secret depression that is rooted in economics that many Black men battle. It is hidden underneath an assortment of layers including an exaggerated bravado, drug and alcohol abuse, misdirected anger, and other forms of destructive behavior. Fantastical illusions are also a tool that is deployed to cope with the humbling realities of an often-marginalized existence.

The "Bow Wow Challenge" that took over social media a few years ago was a reflection of a daily pattern of illusions for many. Some aspect of the rapper and actor "Bow Wow" fronting like he was traveling on a private plane instead of his actual reality of flying coach on a commercial airline is frequently in operation for Black people in this country.

For all of the trips, fancy purses, and Jordan-brand shoes the truth is that the vast majority of people are barely scraping by. Credit, celebrities, and trinkets have given many of us the illusion that we are doing much better economically than we actually are. We have been bamboozled by Facebook likes, hoodwinked by Instagram comments, and led astray by Twitter retweets. Social media has a tendency to tell you a lot of things that aren't true.

The data suggest that the majority of African Americans are not in a great place financially. A prime example of this is a finding from the "The Color of Wealth in Boston" report that found that the median net worth of White households in Boston is $247,500 while the median net worth of Black households is $8 (Munoz et. al, 2015).

The average net worth of a single Black woman with a bachelor's degree is $-11,000 and the median wealth of a single Black woman without a bachelor's degree is $0 (Zaw et al.). This underscores the sad reality that getting a college degree may actually be a hindrance in some cases to a person's wealth position because of the frequent need to go into large amounts of debt in order to obtain higher education.

Most of the racial wealth gaps that exist are a result of the lack of intergenerational wealth transfers available for Black families based on a host of different reasons ranging from Federal Housing Administration policy, slavery, Jim Crowe laws, employment discrimination, denial of access to capital, and the list goes on and on.

The larger point in citing these figures is that we are economically struggling because we began a figurative 100-meter dash 50 meters behind. There is an economic disadvantage for Blacks that is built into the fabric of American society. We don't need to beat ourselves up in a desire to keep up with "the Joneses". This doesn't mean that you shouldn't strive for excellence in every realm, but it does mean that killing yourself to try to keep up with images that may or may not be real will only lead to a life of frustration.

Black men are particularly susceptible to this kind of unhealthy pressure and stress. As they have grown into adulthood, they have seen many of their childhood dreams deferred. Jay Z articulated this in his song Izzo (H.O.V.A.) when he said "I've seen hoop dreams deflate like a true fiend's weight." You will frequently see people holding onto their dreams of being rap stars or NBA players well into their 30s or even 40s. It is a good thing in one sense to hold on to your dream, but the limited number of slots in those arenas suggests than many of these dreams will eventually be shattered.

The lack of a viable "Plan B" in the form of education, job training, or entrepreneurial expertise stymies some from progression. Others have gone and acquired credentials, but still seem to be locked out of gainful economic opportunity. When viable economic options are taken off of the table, then people are more apt to turn to criminal endeavors to meet immediate survival needs for them and their families.

Black men are the most unemployed and incarcerated group in the country per capita. The jobless rate for Black men between ages of 20 and 34 in many cities including Chicago,

Philadelphia, Detroit, and Baltimore is above 45% according to the U.S. Census Bureau's American Community Survey.

The psychological impact on men who haven't been able to overcome the reality of the labor market is a story that is seldom told. Many are suffering from broken dreams and delusions of grandeur that have not been fulfilled. An argument can be made that many Black men have been suffering from a secret depression for years as a result of this financial crunch. A great deal of it probably has its roots in an economic struggle.

I am not licensed to give a diagnosis of depression, but I can give you some reasons that Black men may feel bad about themselves. The first is the sense of inadequacy that comes with being unstable to fulfill the traditional role of being the provider for their family. This may lead to a loss in admiration and respect from their spouse or partner that can chip away at one's self-esteem.

In some cases, women have been openly disrespectful towards a man who is unable to fulfill core financial needs. This is undoubtedly a contributor to high divorce rates. A lack of financial stability can furthermore cause single men to not even want to engage in the dating process. The dating scene often involves the man having to pick up the tab for expensive meals and entertainment activities.

There is a mask of false bravado that many men wear. Underneath the mask, they are hurting because they haven't figured out a way to live up to an ever-elusive standard set by a hyper-materialistic American society. The standard is not one set amount of financial accumulation, but an ever-changing goal line that seems to always be just out of reach.

There is also the specter of social media that often causes

people to act like they are in a financial position that is not in alignment with their reality. The point when the reality sets in that they are not the "baller" that they portray on social media can potentially create an impostor syndrome that can lead to deeper levels of depression.

The realities of the labor market cannot be ignored. Black men have almost been rendered as obsolete in some areas of employment. Many of the traditional factory jobs that Black men once occupied have disappeared due to a myriad of factors, including globalization, automation, and competition from immigrant groups. A significant number of people have taken to self-medicating themselves with drugs and alcohol to cope with their frustration and disappointment.

Rural areas that are predominately White are now being hit with the consequences of economic deterioration that has impacted inner cities for decades. The stress of being unable to adequately meet financial obligations has the capacity to press almost anyone into destructive behaviors. There has been a good deal written about the heroin and opioid crisis in various regions of the country. It has been hypothesized that a sizable portion of the crisis can be attributed to undiagnosed depression.

Solutions for Broken Dreams and Financial Illusions: The Secret Depression of Black Men

The consequences of decades of economic marginality go beyond what meets the eye. It cuts deep beneath the surface. The pressure and frustration that people are feeling are very real. We have to be honest about our economic situation in order to generate the kind of attention, energy, and focus needed to address it. No amount Instagram flauging can override the actual wealth data that encapsulates our situation in hard numbers. As racial wealth gap guru Antonio Moore reported in a Newsmax article, the median Black family is worth $1,700 (Moore, 2017). We can't address the problems in a collective manner until we are honest about our situation.

This is not an all-encompassing set of recommendations, but rather a mix of policy, personal, and community actions that can help to move us forward. A somewhat broad overview of some important topics is listed below. More in-depth inquiries into each of these topics will be forthcoming in future articles.

Encourage Flexible Credit Requirements for Homeownership

Homeownership has historically been one of the key wealth building vehicles in American society. The intentional efforts of the Federal Housing Administration to cut off avenues of home purchasing, restrict areas where Blacks could buy, and subsidize the development of Whites-only communities has contributed enormously to the racial wealth gap that we see today.

One of the biggest barriers to homeownership today for Blacks is inflexible credit requirements for reasonable interest rates on home mortgages. A more flexible credit evaluation that takes other measures into account would responsibly expand access to homeownership for millions of Americans. The numbers suggest Blacks are much less likely to have any reserve funds available in the case of an emergency. Most are living paycheck to paycheck. Thus, when the inevitable "rainy days" come their credit is likely to be adversely affected.

The report entitled "A Policy Agenda for Closing the Racial Wealth Gap" recommended the use of "alternative credit models rather than relying on the exclusive use of FICO scores for homeownership credit assessments." The models use "use alternative risk profiles such as rent, childcare, utilities, and medical care to better understand a client's risk-taking behavior" (Center for Global Policy Solutions, 2016).

Contracts and Workforce Participation

The area with arguably the greatest level of potential for the expansion of large-scale economic opportunity is public sector contracts and development initiatives. Public entities spend billions of dollars a year on different projects and services. There should be a renewed focus on how these dollars are distributed. Communities should be asking what percentage of public contracts in the city go to Black-owned companies? What percentage of the workforce is Black for the companies that get the contracts? How does that match up with the percentage of Blacks in the area?

You have to have data in order to address this issue. Elected officials should use their leverage to assist in the acquisition and promotion of this data. The percentage of Blacks who get contracts and who get jobs on publicly funded projects does not even come close to the percentage of the Black population in most cities. This must be addressed if the beleaguered economic predicament of communities of color is to change.

Focus Buying Power and Partner on Entrepreneurial Ventures

Channeling our buying power will also be a key to increasing economic opportunity.The general lack of access to capital in Black communities serves as a deterrent for many from attempting to start business enterprises and engaging in entrepreneurial pursuits. It will be necessary to expand our tradition of making a lot out of a little and finding creative ways to sustain and excel.

Many successful business owners will often tell grand stories about how their success is attributable to their business acumen and expertise. The story that they seldom tell is exactly how they get the initial capital to launch their businesses.

Blacks are much less likely to be able to call upon family members to gift them the substantial amount of money that is often required to start and sustain successful businesses. The lack of familial wealth causes some to garner the initial capital to operate businesses by any means necessary. We must find multiple means to pool our resources to build an independent economic base. Some models that have shown some success are co-ops and small business incubators.

The unintended consequence of integration was the death of many Black-owned businesses. Blacks began to patronize White-owned establishments more frequently after the barriers were lifted, but it was not reciprocated by Whites for the most part. The Black community relinquished a great deal of their economic empowerment and autonomy as we were more integrated in American society. In retrospect, a more balanced approach that didn't include a large-scale abandonment of Black businesses and institutions would have been more prudent.

Let us learn from the failures and successes of the past to lay the foundation for the long-term contributions to a more vibrant and potent economic base where people feel like they have to capitulate to injustice and inequity to survive financially.

Increase Financial Literacy

Increasing our level of financial literacy can only help our predicament. I admittedly had a low level of financial literacy, which contributed to the deepening of some financial holes.

Unfortunately, basic principles of financial literacy like the impact of credit, investing in the stock market, retirement funds, etc. are not taught in schools on a broad level. We should push for this to be added to the school curriculum and to be emphasized with families and communities.

It must be emphasized, however, that financial literacy alone is not an adequate solution to economic marginalization. It is one piece of a much larger set of policies and practices that should be revamped. Contrary to popular belief, studies show that Blacks actually save at a higher rate than their White counterparts. It is other factors like inheritance, money transfers, and other unearned benefits that made the bulk of the difference. Economists have estimated that up to eighty percent of the wealth that is accumulated during a lifetime can be directly attributed to past generations (inheritances, transfers, etc.) (Rockeymoore & Guzman, 2014).

Avoid Huge College Debt If You Can

I ran up a tremendous amount of debt in the process of getting my Ph.D. Because of this, I want to caution people to avoid huge student loan debt if you can. The need for people to obtain a post-secondary education of some kind is abundantly clear. Most of the new jobs that will be created will require some kind of higher education. It is imperative, however, for those considering higher education opportunities to investigate a multitude of different options to get that additional schooling and take cost into account.

We cannot continue to make the mistake of majoring in anything and blindly going into enormous amounts of debt, assuming that we will get some lucrative opportunity to pay that debt off in the future. Thousands of college students are graduating and either finding themselves unemployed or severely underemployed. This is especially true for Blacks and Hispanics who are twice as likely to be unemployed and stay jobless for longer periods of time. Additionally, empirical studies have shown that applicants with white sounding names are 50% more likely to get call backs for interviews than applicants with black sounding names (Sanders, 2015).

We also cannot ignore the demands of the labor market when selecting a major. We need to be realistic about the kind of opportunities are likely to be available when we graduate with a degree in a particular field. Too many of us are deluded into believing that there will be an economic "yellow brick road" laid out for us when we graduate. This leads to major disappointment and huge student loan bills.

Push for Immediate Record Expungement

Too many people are prevented from employment opportunities because of a nonviolent offense in their past. Even after they have served their time, they are still on punishment. A biased policing practice that heavily surveils and criminalizes Black men has led to a permanent disadvantage when seeking employment.

The disclosure of a prior criminal record is a disqualifying factor in many cases that even immigrants who come from other countries in search of work don't have to contend with. It is simply not fair to continue to punish an individual who may have served time for a petty drug charge after they have already served their debt to society. There should be a push for legislation to be passed to remove the shackles from these individuals so that they can be freed from an additional barrier that may prevent them from being economically viable.

A more immediate step that can be taken while the longer criminal justice policy reform battles are being waged is the banning of the box on employment applications to prevent employers from considering a person's criminal history until after an offer has been made. Localities can follow the example of cities like Austin, Texas who have put "ban the box" measures in place. Some progress is better than no progress (Gordon & Mora, 2016).

Finally, it is important to value and appreciate who and what you do have. The struggle and pressure of everyday life can be suffocating. It has the capacity to destroy the self-esteem of some and crush the aspirations of others.

Dr. Martin Luther King Jr. who lead the charge for the passage of monumental civil rights legislation also gave us an internal charge that is still relevant today: "Believe in yourself and believe that you are somebody......Nobody else can do this for us, no document can do this for us.....If the Negro is the be free he must move down into the inner resources of his own soul and sign with a pen in the ink of self-asserted manhood his own Emancipation Proclamation.....Don't let anybody take your manhood."

How the "San Franciscoization" of More Cities Threatens Student Retention and Graduation Prospects

"They're people with jobs. They're people who work full-time and still can't afford to live in the city. San Francisco is moving fast. Entire neighborhoods are changing. And thousands of people are being left behind" (Lien, 2022). This quote comes from a Vox article entitled "Inside San Francisco's housing crisis" and it is indicative of what is going on in an increasing number of places across the country.

While there is no doubt that the city has wonderful elements to it that include great culture, diversity, unique architecture, creativity, and fabulous restaurants. The "San Franciscoization" of an increasing number of cities is spreading a set of housing circumstances that was once confined to a smaller number of areas to many more.

The San Franciscoization term refers to an assortment of factors associated with a several lack of quality housing that is affordable that includes skyrocketing rent and a housing market that is financially out of reach for most Americans.

Housing instability is an issue for students that has always been a factor for a segment of the population but may explode to a larger portion in short order if current trends continue. Explosions in the cost of housing are causing financial states of emergency in households across the country. The social, mental, and physical consequences of this are devastating.

As eviction moratoriums expire and other forms of housing support evaporate or languish; the fate of students and families hang in balance. The plight of those who are trying to figure out how they are going to maintain some semblance of a material quality of life is deserving of care, concern, and attention.

If one doesn't have a stable place to live; then they clearly aren't in the optimal circumstances needed to perform at a consistently high academic level. This is one of the main issues that lie beneath poor retention numbers. The context of unaffordable housing and the economic deprivation that far too many students face is crucial and must be addressed in an expeditious manner.

The bottom line is that as housing costs have soared, wages have not. This has placed a tremendous amount of financial pressure on many families who may be renting or don't have any form of consistent housing at all. The need for governmental intervention at the federal, state, and local levels is clear.

The current trajectory is unsustainable in general and has a direct impact on higher education. This is especially pertinent for predominantly commuter schools who either have no student housing or a very limited amount of housing on campus. Institutions should work with local agencies, elected officials, and other entities to find solutions for students and figure out ways to provide support for their housing needs.

If left unaddressed, retention and completion rates are likely to fall even more as students may be forced to dropout due to stress derived from having to figure out where they will lay their head on a nightly basis, taking on more jobs that reduce needed academic time, or severe academic underperformance due to a redirected focus on basic survival.

This issue should be treated like a state of emergency and addressed head on in a consistent manner for a sustained change to take place where a significant number of students are better able to maximize their academic potential without having to contend with the heavy burden of housing insecurity and constantly scrambling for basic shelter and a place to stay.

The Economic Aspect of Police Officer Involved Tragedies Cannot Be Overlooked

The economic aspect of several tragedies involving law enforcement officials cannot be overlooked amidst the calls for reform of policing practices. In many ways, the economic status of minority communities is inextricably linked to the plight of Blacks and Hispanics in the criminal justice system.

The 2016 killing of Alton Sterling in Baton Rouge highlighted again the over policing of petty infractions like selling CDs that people are engaged in to try to feed their families in environments where economic opportunity has been depleted. The need for an economic stimulus plan for communities of color is extreme. Blacks have become a permanent underclass in many cities and the underground economy has become the only economy for too many. Sustained community pressure must be exerted in order to create economic opportunity.

In an atmosphere of gridlock at the Congressional level, we must look to the local level to bring about tangible change. We must be deliberate and strategic when tackling systemic problems. An increased emphasis on measures like increasing the minimum wage and requiring a greater representation of minority owned vendors in government contracting will improve economic opportunity in areas that desperately need it. Another step is to gather diversity data on who every major corporation in your area is employing and contracting. We don't have an obligation to spend money where we can't work or get contracts.

There is a need for communities to know the diversity data for the major corporations in their areas. The placement of one or two highly placed Blacks is not the solution. They are often under pressure to be docile and non-threatening to the existing status quo. These few individuals are often limited in their ability to effect change from the inside. The pressure must come from the outside.

We need to go beyond discussions on race and deal with an

economic system that people of color have largely been locked out of. If we don't deal with this using data, we will ultimately be spinning our wheels with only anecdotal guidance and the conditions of our communities will not change. There is less crime in economically empowered communities and thus less of a perception of people in the community as criminals.

This is particularly evident in communities that are occupied by police officers that live outside of the areas that they are policing. A significant problem is that many officers are scared of the people that they are sworn to serve and protect a lot of that is based on perception. The perception is based on a racial bias that views blacks as criminals. The numbers suggest that there is a predisposition of criminal intent at every level.

The "just get an education" tactic is not sufficient. Black college graduates are twice as likely to be unemployed. Hispanic graduates are two thirds as likely to be unemployed (Douglas-Gabriel, 2015). Black and Hispanics are also out of work 7-9 additional weeks. Additionally, empirical studies have shown that job applicants with white sounding names are 50% more likely to get call backs for interviews than applicants with black sounding names (Sanders, 2015).

Yes, we need to get more people in job training programs and institutions of higher education, but even more work needs to be done to open up the doors to economic prosperity. Corporations should be pressured to put jobs and contracts on the table.

There also needs to be a renewed effort to educate minority students on entrepreneurship and how to build businesses. Many students have only been taught to be employees and are therefore perpetually reduced to having to beg the dominant society to give them access to a job.

Along with the need for more people to learn how to build businesses is the need to remove barriers to access startup capital. Blacks are much less likely to have transformative assets passed down to them. They were excluded from many vehicles of intergenerational wealth transfer that were used to build the middle class through methods like redlining and the exclusion of the majority of Blacks during the first decades of Social Security.

This intergenerational wealth transfer can be seen in the form of inheritance, trust funds, college payments, down payments for houses, private school payments, credit card payments, medical bills, access to capital, and business startup money. The tremendous economic and community wealth ramifications that Black communities feel today can be traced to government policy and practices that have led to systemic disadvantage.

Singing kumbuya together at a peace rally is wonderful, but it won't change the day-to-day reality in our communities. Along with protesting we must do the due diligence to formulate and implement a strategy that will bring about a lasting change.

Where is the Diversity and Inclusion in Higher Education Engagement with Investment Management Firms?

The question of how equitable the engagement of higher education institutions with private equity firms and other investment management groups is a difficult one to answer. The reason for this is that there is an incredible lack of transparency in identifying what money managers many higher education institutions are using to steward their endowments.

The Knight Foundation's 2021 report that sought to examine the diversity of the asset managers for the wealthiest 50 public and private universities had 34 of the institutions decline to participate. These institutions have a combined $273 billion under management (Knight Foundation, 2022). The key question is, who is managing these assets?

The fact is that many higher education institutional endowments and pension plans more broadly have significant percentages of students and personnel of color that pay into these vehicles on a regular basis. Many of these institutions hand out these funds to investment firms across the country. These funds do not equitably go to Black and Hispanic owned firms. It seems that people of color are good enough to put their money into the system, but they aren't perceived as being good enough to manage the assets.

One result is that Black and Hispanic owned firms are frequently not able to raise funds that are as big as their counterparts. Thus, many are denied greater opportunities to increase their capacity to make meaningful investments in communities that they have direct connection to.

There is also the false narrative of having make a tradeoff between diversity and performance. Multiple reports have found that there is no evidence of being a reduced level of performance in utilizing diverse money managers (Correa, 2021). Diversity has been shown to be an enhancer of performance in many cases (Weinberg & Greer, 2017).

New pipelines of opportunity for diverse investment managers are needed to break into areas where little to no diversity has historically existed. The aforementioned report from the Knight Foundation cited some reasons for why asset manager rosters can be slow to change including "asset managers' intentionally long-term investment objectives and processes, established relationships with current managers, low manager turnover and the need for extensive due diligence before hiring new managers" (Knight Foundation, 2022, p. 11).

One recommendation that was put forth by the Diverse Asset Managers Initiative in a guide related to investing with diverse asset managers is to utilize the "Rooney Rule" that is used in the National Football League (NFL) for the hiring of head coaches and general managers (Weinberg & Greer, 2017). The rule requires that teams "conduct an in-person interview with at least one external minority candidate for any GM or head coaching interview" among other requirements (National Football League, n.d., Strengthening The Rooney Rule section). This could also be used for decisions regarding investment firm selections by colleges and universities for money management.

Weinberg and Greer (2017) also highlighted the fact that the state of Illinois already has the Rooney Rule language in its legislation. It reads: "if in any case an emerging investment manager meets the criteria established by a board for a specific search and meets the criteria established by a consultant for that search, then that emerging investment manager shall receive an invitation by the board of trustees, or an investment committee of the board of trustees, to present his or her firm for final consideration of a contract. In the case where multiple emerging investment managers meet the criteria of this section, the staff may choose the most qualified firm or firms to present to the board."

There is also a need for greater efforts to build more diverse talent pipelines into the investment banking and private equity industry. A piece entitled "PE Firms Are Making Diversity

Efforts, But It Will Likely Be a Long Road" by Hannah Zhang asserted that private equity has lagged behind other areas of the finance sector when it comes to diversity stating that "according to a recent Ernst & Young report, only 3 percent of employees in the PE industry are Black, compared with 12 percent at banks. Among the portfolio companies backed by the top 18 PE firms and venture capitalists, only 2 percent of board seats are held by Black and Latino directors" (Zhang, 2021, para. 3).

Just as higher education institutions should increase their level of transparency when it comes to who is managing their endowments, investment management firms should have transparency in their recruiting, hiring, promotion, and workforce diversity status.

One step forward would be for firms to better articulate what knowledge, skills, ability, competencies, credentials, and intangible factors are needed to attain roles at every level of the organization. This would provide some clearly defined targets for people to prepare, train, and shoot for. The bar does not have to be lowered for diversity to flourish, it just needs to be made clear and people of different backgrounds need to be given a fair chance to compete.

There are some entry-level roles at many firms that college and university graduates can move right into if they have been properly groomed through their coursework and potential internships, apprenticeships, or work experience. There is a need for an increased level of intentionality to be injected throughout the development and maintenance of career pathways in private equity and investment banking. This entails being deliberative and specific regarding the creation of opportunities for both preparation and advancement.

Support along the journey from initial exposure to the securing of upper echelon positions is critical to facilitating breakthroughs for people who historically have been denied the opportunity to ascend to certain career heights in sizable numbers. Putting qualified and capable people and firms on the radar of those who make both hiring decisions at firms and selections of investment managers for college and university endowments is an important step towards the creation of a more equitable landscape for higher education engagement with asset management groups.

Career Mobility

Fear of the Gaze: How Perceived Judgement Impacts Student Career Choices

W.E.B. DuBois in *The Souls of Black Folk* described the Negro as being "born with a veil and gifted with a second-sight in this American world, - a world which yields him no true self-consciousness but only lets him see himself through the revelation of the other world. It is a peculiar sensation, this double-consciousness, this sense of always looking at one's self through the eyes of others of measuring one's soul by the tape of a world that looks on in amused contempt and pity."

The other world that DuBois describes is what this piece will refer to as "the gaze". It is an expansion of the concept of the "white gaze" that the poet Toni Morrison popularized, but the gaze in this context applies to individuals regardless of their race, religion, gender, ethnicity, or sexual orientation. The gaze is the external evaluation or judgement that people feel from others and the broader society at large. The fear of being judged is something that everyone must contend with to a certain extent. It is applicable across multiple sectors and populations.

The way in which one addresses this fear can play a large role in the routes that they decide to pursue and the manner that they go about doing it. An overemphasis on perceived judgement from the gaze can cause a severe misalignment between one's purpose and career path. The concept of "people pleasing" ties in here. Psychology Today describes people pleasers as those who "decide that everyone else's needs are more pressing than their own. They put themselves on the back burner in their own lives, and then end up feeling resentful, dissatisfied, and depressed" (Smyth, 2020). The root of it is that they live in fear of being disliked and this can become a psychological prison of limiting beliefs that prevent them from living their best life.

The tipping point can be when the fear of being perceived by the gaze in a certain way causes one to retreat from going all out in the pursuit of their aims. This fear-based mindset leads to a limiting decision-making process when it comes to people believing that they can attain certain goals. The practical implications of this are that it can cause higher education institutions, corporations, and other organizations to experience high levels of employee turnover, alienation, low workplace morale, and an overall prevalence of underachievement.

It can start at young ages when children abandon their dreams and desired career paths because it may not be deemed as valuable by others. This starts a pattern of people judging themselves based on the value assessment of the external gaze. If awareness of this pattern is not highlighted, then one can get caught up in a perpetual cycle of discontent chasing a constantly moving measuring stick of approval and validation from the gaze.

A key internal question for people to ask themselves is are they doing what they are doing because they really want to or are they doing it solely to get approval from the gaze? There can be a continual search for validation and proving oneself as "worthy" in the eyes of who one sees as a "validator". These validators have been given power over some portion of the person's sense of their own worthiness. There are no doubt members of the gaze who will matter more than others to an individual like one's significant other, children, and parents, but even the views of those loved ones can be detrimental if they exceed the power of one's own definition of themselves.

When one relinquishes the power of their own definition to others then they are subject to the whims of external marginalization and limitations that they have made agreement with by virtue of the abdication of their own power to define themselves. A sizable part of the potency of the gaze involves how much power one gives over to certain people outside of themselves to define who they are. A potential negative consequence of this is living a fear-based life to appease others where students waste money, time, and resources going into fields that they had no desire to go into. The pursuit of trying to prove oneself worthy of validation from the gaze can cause significant deviations from one's true passion and purpose.

Increasing awareness of the gaze on the front end of career path decisions can lay the foundation for significant levels of achievement and satisfaction in the long run. Providing people with tools and strategies to help them bring into alignment how they act both inside and outside of the gaze is key to freeing individuals from the fear of external condemnation or disapproval. There is a need to embed curriculum and processes within educational systems that will support the inner development of people to fortify themselves against the growing influence of negative side effects of the gaze. This will help to build up a refusal of people to be bounded by the limitations that others or the broader society try to thrust on them.

Everyone desires external appreciation and recognition for their efforts and being on some level. It can help to motivate heightened levels of individual and collective achievement. It can be a positive compliment to a solid internal foundation of self-worth, self-valuation, and self-esteem.

A key is sustaining one's belief in their ability to succeed in a certain course regardless of what members of the external gaze prescribe to their ability or potential. This requires the cultivation of a high level of resistance against the potential "people pleasing" pattern of suppressing of one's true self and conforming to the confines of external limitations. The challenge is to not be controlled by the gaze and to develop an inner peace that cannot be altered by external factors.

Our society is set up to try to categorize people and put them in boxes. There is a constant external evaluation and validation process. The gaze will declare you as a winner or a loser if you allow it to. You have the power to elect yourself as the President of your own environment. You have the power of agency and self-governance unless you decide to give it away. The choice is yours.

Sunken Place University

Carter G. Woodson wrote in his book The Mis-Education of the Negro that "if you can control a man's thinking you don't have to worry about his action. When you determine what a man shall think you do not have to concern yourself about what he will do. If you make a man feel that he is inferior, you do not have to compel him to accept an inferior status, for he will seek it himself. If you make a man think that he is justly an outcast, you do not have to order him to the back door. He will go without being told; and if there is no back door, his very nature will demand one."

The underlying theme of the hit movie "Get Out" is about a mind control process that conditions Black people to accept a marginalized status and continually choose to go into the back doors of life. This mentality of consistently accepting a second-class placement permeates many colleges, universities, and other educational institutions.

The broader context of the movie is the interaction between the Black male main character, Chris, and the White family of the young lady (Rose) that he was dating. Unbeknownst to Chris, he had been selected to enter a system of mental programming that was designed to detach him from the community and consciousness that he came from.

The movie featured a pivotal scene where Chris was hypnotized by the mother of Rose. Upon being hypnotized, he fell into a place that was described as "the Sunken Place." Jordan Peele, the film's director, recently tweeted that "The Sunken Place means we're marginalized. No matter how hard we scream, the system silences us." This description is particularly relevant to certain college and university personnel.

Many institutions have Sunken Place-like settings that cause some Black employees to operate in an atmosphere of fear and weakness. They do this by incentivizing and rewarding those who comport themselves as docile and non-threatening. This is what causes highly placed Blacks in universities and school systems to frequently remain silent about rampant inequality and ineptness.

The hypnotism that Chris underwent is replicated in higher education every day. People are hypnotized by a position or a title. They are hypnotized by being accepted as a "good Negro" in the dominant society. They are hypnotized by a fear of being punished for upsetting the status quo.

Though these individuals may be benefitting themselves, they are essentially a disgrace to the broader community. They have bought into an incomplete notion of "success" based on an inadequate system-generated measuring stick that prizes private gain over systemic change.

Many have bought into the selfish notion of individual advancement without caring about community upliftment. Economic dependency on the system then makes individuals capitulate to whatever the system desires in order to survive and pay bills. If one were to break free from the unconscious "Sunken Place" state, they would be risking the possibility of not being able to provide for your family. Thus, the system seldom changes to a significant degree and even those highly placed individuals who are bold and outspoken behind closed doors end up being silent when it really matters.

There are many other people trapped in the lower levels of organizations that feel that they are never given a chance. This is a different kind of "Sunken Place." Those people who are in this predicament must find alternative ways to exercise their gifts and talents so that they can reach a level of self-actualization that ultimately brings a deep sense of fulfillment. The kind of fulfillment that comes with tapping into their potential and using their ability to positively impact the world and make a difference.

The ultimate question for highly placed persons in higher education institutions is how uncomfortable they are willing to get. Can they survive rocking the boat and upsetting the status quo? Can they cultivate the fearlessness that is missing from the majority of higher education executives?

It is this elusive fearlessness and willingness to take some risks that will free people from Sunken Place University and allow them to get out of a life of being boxed in. It is time to resist falling into the vast abyss of becoming the typical walking zombie who feels like they will lose their job if they have any semblance of a backbone.

We can no longer afford for people to stay silent in Sunken Places and allowing themselves to be put into a box every day where their ability is marginalized, suppressed, and buried. This is the time for people to come out from behind their cubicles and push the envelope on issues that matter to them. Effective leadership is not in the center, it is on the edge. We must find a way to "Get Out."

Frozen Place University

"It's not easy for me to admit that I've been standing in the same place for 18 years." – Troy Maxson in the Movie "Fences" (played by Denzel Washington)

I have written about the concept of "The Sunken Place" as was portrayed in the movie "Get Out". I referred to The Sunken Place as being a mind control process that conditions Black people to accept a marginalized status and continually choose to go into the back doors of life. Jordan Peele, the film's director, tweeted in the aftermath of the film that "The Sunken Place means we're marginalized. No matter how hard we scream, the system silences us" (Peele, 2017).

This piece will lay out some of the characteristics of a "Frozen Place" that many people find themselves in on their career journeys. The Frozen Place is when a person feels like they are stuck in a certain position or station and unable to progress. They may stay "frozen" for years with little to no upward mobility or growth. In the Frozen Place, career stagnation is the norm. There are those who have not been able to advance despite their hard work and education. They, like Troy in the movie Fences, feel stuck in place.

There are those people who encounter glass doors where they are denied access to positions regardless of their education, experience, and credentials. The doors are made of glass because they can see others with an equivalent or lower levels of qualifications gaining access to opportunities in institutions and organizations that they could not. For those who do get in the door, there may be glass ceiling that restricts how high they can climb.

Those individuals who are in the Frozen Place may end up feeling unfulfilled and may seek other often destructive ways to fill the void. Their life doesn't come close to meeting the aspirations and expectations that they once had. Eventually, the disappointment of not meeting their expectations can take a toll on the person. The result is often a perpetually negative attitude and outlook that ends up causing them to sink deeper into a mental abyss.

The Frozen Place makes people feel like they have no upward mobility. Many occupants of this space have stopped trying to live out their ambitions and have settled into an unenthusiastic life of mundanity and mediocrity. They feel that no matter what they do, they're going nowhere. This may result in a complete loss of enthusiasm for their job. These individuals go into a zombie-like state when they enter their workplaces.

They just go through the motions every day and go home. Their motivation has all but ceased. There is really no career path in the minds of these individuals. They have learned to suppress their ambitions and muffle their dreams. The fire that they may have once had has been extinguished. They are increasingly susceptible to being paralyzed by fear, crushed by roadblocks, and frozen by pessimism.

People in the Frozen Place are likely to feel powerless and totally at the mercy of their employer. They will sit in dead-end jobs for years because they don't feel like they can get anything else. They see the number of people who are unemployed and feel a sense of gratitude for just having a job, but this limited satisfaction causes them to just settle for where they are and ignore their dreams and passion.

The Frozen Place encapsulates a perceived inability to escape one's social location and positioning. Social positions refer to who is participating and who is not as well as the level of participation in terms of who is allowed to move up. Even if they like the mission of the organization or the entity, they may feel like they have to leave it in order to achieve any semblance of self-actualization where they feel like they are operating in their gifts and maximizing their talent.

The Frozen Place can create an exaggerated sense of contentment and comfort in some cases. Those who are frozen are typically afraid of change. These people feel safe in their roles and don't want to "rock the boat". Comfort, however, can lead to stagnation after a period of time. Individuals may feel that if they venture out, then they will fail.

There is also a segment of people who once were "go getters", but have stopped striving for more over the course of time. The Frozen Place is not necessarily where you are positioned, but it is complete acceptance of your position. You are in the Frozen Place when you have stopped striving.

Institutions can help individuals thaw out of their Frozen Place by providing them with some "antifreeze". They can clarify potential career paths and offer multiple avenues for advancement. People that occupy Frozen Places may also need to go back to school to get new skill sets to help to unfreeze themselves. Many of them have the ability, but they are waiting for someone to give them permission to use it. There are unnecessary restrictions that they put on themselves.

The best antifreeze is options and versatility. The ability to take advantage of opportunities in a number of different arenas is vital because a person can always get frozen out of one particular area. When one avenue is blocked then it is necessary to turn onto other streets that also go in the direction of one's desired destination.

If you are in the Frozen Place, it's not too late to change your mindset in order to pull out buried knowledge, skills, and ability that may be buried and guide it in the right direction. You have the capacity and opportunity to defrost yourself out and run toward your dreams.

The Jalen Hurts Template on How to Handle Career Storms

There are lessons from college sports that can be transferred to other areas of life, even to higher educational administrative apparatuses. Personnel moves on the football field can mirror personnel moves in departments or schools. People are put in different positions and called upon to execute different roles and assignments.

The people who are moved are not emotionless robots, but human beings who feel, think, and have their own personal aspirations in addition to the goals of a particular entity. This can make personnel moves complicated and multi-dimensional. A poorly thought out move that doesn't take a multitude of factors into account can destroy the atmosphere of a working environment and foster division instead of collaboration. There is responsibility on both those who make the decisions and those who are impacted by those decisions.

The COVID-19 pandemic has created a new onslaught of organizational redesigns, demotions, pay cuts, layoffs, resignations, and firings. Each of these can create significant disruptions for the operating efficiency and effectiveness of organizations. A great example of how to handle a demotion and career redirection was provided by former University of Alabama Quarterback Jalen Hurts.

Hurts began his career at Alabama as the backup Quarterback. He became the starter after performing well in his first game in replacement of the starting quarterback Blake Barnett after he had been pulled out by Head Coach Nick Saban. Hurts went on to lead the Crimson Tide to a victory over the University of Southern California Trojans.

He would remain the starter and lead the Crimson Tide to the National Championship game where they eventually lost in overtime to a Clemson University team led by quarterback Deshaun Watson. Hurts had a stellar season and was named the

Southeastern Conference (SEC) Offensive Player of the Year and Freshman of the Year. Hurts would again lead Alabama back to the National Championship game as a starter during his sophomore season.

Though they were winning games during the year, some glaring holes in Hurts' game were beginning to show and be exploited by opposing teams. He was an outstanding runner and leader of his teammates, but his passing performance was inconsistent and needed significant improvement.

This weakness finally caught up with him as the opposing Georgia Bulldogs had his Alabama Crimson Tide team down 13 to 0 at halftime of the 2018 National Championship Game. At that point Hurts was benched in favor of the more dynamic passer Tua Tagovailoa. Tagovailoa led Alabama to an exhilarating comeback victory that was capped off by a game winning touchdown pass. Hurts outwardly congratulated Tagovailoa and celebrated with his teammates but must have felt some sense of dejection at the same time.

Hurts would say later in an ESPN interview that reflected on the game that the "day made me who I am, I wouldn't change it for the World." Most people will never have to deal with that kind of public demotion in front of millions of people, but they will deal with some level of harsh critique, role reduction, dismissal, or career redirection.

It can cause an identity crisis for those who have identified a lot of themselves with their job. It can cause one to question their own value, ability, and purpose. It can be extremely disappointing to invest a great deal of one's life into a certain job only to be discarded or pushed aside.

The COVID-19 pandemic shut down entire industries and

caused massive employment losses and downsizing. The trend of human jobs being lost to automation only accelerated more. The numbers of those who have been let go have been widely reported, but there is also a need to go beyond the numbers and look at the human impact.

It would be prudent for those who have been impacted by this kind of career adversity to study how Jalen Hurts handled the loss of his starting role. Tagovailoa had replaced Hurts as the starting quarterback. Hurts could have pouted and thrown himself a pity party because of his demotion. Instead, stayed the course and took the time to evaluate his game and work on his weaknesses. He supported his teammates and continued to be a team leader from a reserve role. He learned how to lead from behind.

He worked and prepared himself for the next opportunity that he would have to play. He made the most of the time that he did get in games. He held his cards close to his chest so even if he was disgruntled in some way, he didn't show it externally. He could have transferred right away after learning that Tagovailoa would be the starter for the following season, but he stayed with the team and used the time to improve.

In the college football playoffs the next year against Georgia, Hurts would come in for Tagovailoa after he was sidelined by an injury and lead the Crimson Tide to a victory. By the time that Hurts did transfer to another football program a year later at the University of Oklahoma, he was a significantly better player in every area.

His unprecedented demotion after leading Alabama to a 26 (wins) and 2 (losses) record and two consecutive national championship games ultimately catapulted him into becoming a significantly improved version of himself. He arrived at the University of Oklahoma as a far superior quarterback than he was at any point in his Alabama career. This momentum carried him through a standout final college and exceptional rookie season with the NFL's Philadelphia Eagles where he was named the starter during the latter part of the season.

The mindset and strategies that Hurts employed can be utilized by others in different fields who are facing similar career storms. A person can do all the storm preparation in the world, but one only truly knows the quality of their preparation when it is put to the test during a storm. Those who are truly prepared and made deep investments in themselves will be fortified during a storm, those who did not will be blown away.

It is clear that Hurts and his support system made many internal investments in him that fortified his character so that he would be able to sustain and get better during his career storm. Periods of adversity can make or break a person. The wise use the time to do a thorough self-evaluation and confront those areas within themselves where they feel insecure, inadequate, incompetent, or inconsistent. They use these periods to dig deep and discover characteristics about themselves that they may not have known. Follow the Jalen Hurts template when dealing with career storms and make the shift from being a victim to a victor.

Three Powerful Ways to Honor Dr. Martin Luther King Jr. in Our Work

1. Work for a cause that is greater than your career.

Everyone cares about the future direction of their career and wants to be able to make a living for themselves and their families. This sentiment shouldn't be your only driving force. Connect to a cause that is greater than yourself. Find something that you are willing to sacrifice for that will positively impact communities and systems.

In addition to setting a standard of excellence with our behavior; we must also demand excellence and justice in the structural and policy realm. Dr. King gave up a potential career of comfort and convenience to change the laws of the land and help to transform America. After receiving his Ph.D. in 1955, he could have only worried about his personal career growth in the world of academia or the ministry. Instead, he decided to take his talents to Montgomery, Alabama, where he would commit himself to a cause that was greater than himself.

2. Be Courageous.

Dr. King certainly felt fear. In his last speech in Memphis, he lamented that "like anybody, I would like to live a long life. Longevity has its place. But I'm not concerned about that now. I just want to do God's will." King, like all of us, had doubts and fears, but he didn't let that paralyze him. He didn't let it scare him into inaction or passivity. He and many others in the civil rights movement put their jobs and lives on the line. Academics can honor their sacrifice by being courageous.

A great deal of the fear that people feel is self-imposed. They put themselves in cages of trepidation based on what might happen. It must be acknowledged that the majority of scholars of color have been denied intergenerational wealth transfers which makes them much more economically insecure than their counterparts. This, however, is not an excuse for perpetual inaction on pivotal issues. To whom much is given in reference to knowledge, skills, and ability; much is required.

It doesn't mean that you should walk into every meeting screaming "no justice, no peace," but it does mean that you should be applying an equity and access lens to every situation and asking if there is more that can be done.

Another part of being courageous is not always taking the path of least resistance. Dr. King often intentionally chose locations where he would find the most resistance in order to dramatize a particular problem. He intentionally made himself uncomfortable. He went into Birmingham, Selma, Chicago, Memphis, and countless other cities to bring attention to important issues. Academics can help put issues on the agenda with their scholarship and service.

King also wasn't afraid to be controversial. His stance against the Vietnam War caused even some of his closest allies in the civil rights movement to turn against him. During King's final year of life, the heads of the NAACP and National Urban League would denounce him as well as other leading black figures of the time like Congressman Adam Clayton Powell.

Scholars should follow King's lead and venture into some uncharted waters. Put yourself in fearful situations sometimes. It can be an incredible tool for growth. Don't be a Chief Diversity Officer who is afraid to fight for diversity, or a Dean of Equity who consistently stays silent about inequity. It is especially inexcusable for tenured faculty members to be afraid to speak out. Fear has no place in your success equation.

3. Engage.

This is a time for a new level of engagement in both theory and action. Scholars must re-examine theories to gauge their level of relevance to present conditions. We should not settle for conventional solutions to different issues. We should delve deeper into more complex alternatives. The gap between theory and practice will widen if theories aren't reformulated to fit the reality of what is going on.

This is not just a time for analysis, though analysis is important. At some point, the life of the mind needs to connect with the action of the hands and feet. Most scholars essentially write to themselves in academic journals that are not even accessible to the general public. This work is valuable and very highly prized in the academy but may end up being of little use if it is not eventually acted upon.

Academics must find a way to use their scholarship to make the world a better place. Use your skills to change your institutions. Be an agent of institutional transformation. Put your theory into action. Dr. King didn't study Mahatma Ghandi's non-violent tactics just to be studying it. He studied it with the intent of putting it into action. We can honor Dr. King by using our expertise and academic institutions to reach into the community and build coalitions to create opportunity.

Four Career Tips for College Students

I have been asked frequently by students for career advice as I have been conducting career readiness activities across the country. The tips below are written informally and meant to give students a few tangible steps to help them navigate their journey.

1. Begin working on securing employment very early in your program and not at the end.

There will most likely not be a guaranteed job after you graduate. It will be incumbent on you to do everything that you can do to create opportunities for yourself. Secure paid or unpaid internships or part time employment in the field that you want to be in while you are in school. You don't necessarily know what you're getting into if you don't have experience doing it. Even if you have a negative experience, they can be just as informative as positive experiences. We were all told to get good grades and to study hard growing up, but do not expect for your hard work in a classroom setting to immediately translate to the workplace. It is imperative that you mirror your classroom experience with real time work.

With that being said, don't put more on your plate than you can handle. There is no excuse for academic failure. You must have the ability to balance gaining work experience with academic excellence. Gaining relevant experience in your field will give you a competitive advantage in the job market and better prepare you to excel in your role after you attain it.

2. Explore and follow up on multiple career paths in case opportunities in your preferred path are not immediately available.

You want to have the widest array of career options available to you as possible. You may be aiming to secure a career opportunity in a space where there are many people vying for just a few openings. Therefore, you want to position yourself to be able to make a living in an area that is relatively close to your preferred area until a desirable opportunity in your preferred area is available.

3. Constantly focus on how concepts that you learn in your classes can be applied to real life.

I once took a Nonprofit Management course while getting my Master's Degree. I did just enough to get a satisfactory grade and didn't really apply myself to learning the content at the level that I should have. I had no idea at the time that I would find myself at the head of a national nonprofit organization a few years later. I missed the opportunity to be better prepared and more informed to operate as a nonprofit executive.

Do things that are hands on. If your curriculum does not already have activities that are hands on, then you need to take it upon yourself to find training programs that will force you to use these skills hands on. You don't want your first real test to be when your mortgage is on the line.

4. Recognize barriers, but persist in spite of them.

The doors to employment or opportunity can seem to be closed. There are policies and practices that have been deployed at many institutions that have yielded disparate outcomes even if they did not emanate from discriminatory intent. Despite these barriers, you must continue to do everything that is within your capacity to make yourself a more attractive candidate. You can do this by increasing your knowledge, skills, and abilities and putting together a tangible track record of achievement in your field of interest.

Ultimately, we know that education is inextricably linked to economic development. More than half of the new jobs that will be created in the next decade will require some type of post-secondary education. We need you all to continue to pursue knowledge and training, become gainfully employed, and create opportunities either through entrepreneurship or other means for our communities to develop.

Educational Mobility

Uncomfort Zone: Time for Higher Education to Address Race and Class

Pope Paul VI is quoted as saying that "if you want peace, work for justice." Many higher education institutions have made tremendous strides in addressing disparities in the area of race and class. There is, however, a long way to go. Progress without equity is injustice.

Unfortunately, it often takes a crisis for institutions to engage in conversations around race and class. School leadership can lead the charge in being proactive about these issues and bringing these points to the center. If these difficult conversations can't take place at our nation's colleges and universities, then there is little hope for other areas of society.

Colleges that don't address this issue head-on are likely to continue to just apply Band-Aids to deep wounds that don't really address the root of the problems. Interrupting the status quo will require a willingness to get uncomfortable. There is often an unwillingness to have real discussions on sensitive topics because there is a resistance to change in some quarters. There is a reluctance to have real action take place.

The consequences of not addressing the beliefs and issues that lie beneath the surface can be deadly. It is imperative for issues to be out into the open and addressed in a forthright manner. Many people are suffering, but remain silent because they don't want to be labeled as difficult.

Columbia Professor Derald Sue has written extensively about microaggressions and stated that they can be intentional or unintentional. There are those brief interactions that communicate demeaning or hostile messages to members of marginalized groups. We may not even be aware that we are sending these subtle derogatory messages. There is an ever-present need to engage in a self-awareness learning process.

There is a need to cultivate different ways for people to enter the conversation. It may very well be the well-intended actions of good people that are helping to perpetuate inequity in higher education.

It would be prudent for college and university personnel to spend some time excavating and unpacking the hidden messages that are embedded in different interactions. Everyone is capable of delivering and receiving microaggressions because we are all susceptible to taking in the biases and prejudices that are embedded in societal conditioning through a variety of influences.

Microaggressions that continue to go unchecked can eventually become embedded in the culture of the campus. They can reach a level of normalization to where they are taken for granted. The cumulative impact of these interactions can then impact decision making and widen disparities.

Enormous gaps in access and equity have existed so long at some institutions that they no longer raise red flags. It has become a part of standard operating procedure. There is an unwillingness to get uncomfortable and venture into sensitive areas and dynamics that need unpacking.

University leadership can help to inspire faculty to not just focus on tenure, but to put effort towards the transformation of the campus culture. Addressing these disparities in a substantive manner requires something that is often missing

— courage. Speaking up for justice is almost never safe. It is time for colleges and universities to get out of their comfort zones and garner the will to address issues of race and class in a direct manner.

Higher Education Institutions and Civil Rights Groups Should Explore Areas of Convergence

There is plenty of common ground between universities and civil rights groups that needs to be uplifted and utilized. There is a gulf that needs to be filled. Many universities operate as if they are an island unto themselves and many civil rights organizations are as engaged as they could be in the education space. It is becoming increasingly necessary for civil rights groups to work with colleges and universities to increase access to higher education and improve the economic conditions of underserved communities.

There is a natural synergy that needs to be reinforced. There are too many areas of convergence not to. Institutions of higher education should work with civil rights groups to help get their issues on the agenda and have them resonate in the broader public consciousness. Colleges and universities need the consistency of a civil rights organization to help them move issues on the agenda. Otherwise, many issues and concerns will just be an episodic tantrum and the political powers that be can wait them out.

Universities hold the key to the kind of upward mobility and opportunity that the civil rights community has fought to attain for generations. Civil rights organizations need guidance on what to organize around and where to apply public pressure. Higher education institutions can provide that with an increased level of engagement.

Arguably the most pressing area of convergence is the issue of state governments financially starving out public institutions of higher education. The New York Times noted that "since the 2008 recession, states have reduced spending on public higher education by 17 percent per student, while tuition has risen by 33 percent, according to a recent report by the nonpartisan Center on Budget and Policy Priorities" (Chen, 2016, para. 7).

If the current trend of disinvestment goes unmitigated then some states will not end up investing anything towards colleges and universities. This will place an increased burden on poor and working-class students and parents. The process of students gaining access to, and successfully completing programs at institutions of higher education can be long and arduous and does not have the same kind of drama associated with it as police violence but it is as consequential to the long-term sustainability of minority communities.

These issues should remain on the policy agenda and resonate in the public consciousness. The agenda setting process for higher education issues is a key space where the civil rights community should be engaged. Agenda setting refers to the manner in which relatively unknown issues and ideas rise up through different channels to end up under consideration by various areas of the political system at the federal, state, and local levels. Education should be a voting issue in every election.

If higher education institutions and the civil rights community don't collaborate to keep important issues related to post-secondary access and success on the agenda then diminished economic opportunity for minorities will be exacerbated.

Universities have been under increased pressure to further facilitate the process of students obtaining gainful employment after graduating from their institutions (U.S. Department of Education, 2015). There may be a need to pressure corporations to create employment opportunities for students and to invest in higher education institutions.

Another area of convergence that has been increasing brought up by student activists on college campuses and other external stakeholders is the lack of faculty and staff diversity that is prevalent at many universities. If the abysmal faculty diversity numbers of many universities are to change then there must be a serious reexamination of the hiring practices that are currently in existence. There is often a reluctance to address racial issues in the hiring process which leads to a high degree of frustration and discouragement for qualified minority applicants who are never given an opportunity.

Research has highlighted that people typically associate with and are attracted to people who are similar to themselves. This undoubtedly has had a large impact on hiring practices along with a lack of awareness of stereotypes that influence the perception of potential faculty and staff members. The uncomfortable truth is that many diversity officers or highly ranked university officials are hired to help facilitate institutional change, but ultimately end up feeling that the university's leadership is not genuinely supporting their efforts to make that change happen. Many of these people end up with a lot of anguish and frustration and little actual power to alter deeply embedded practices.

In many environments, including universities, there is a denial that issues of privilege, race, and class, even exist and if they do happen to be recognized there is no safe space to break it down and make the appropriate climate changes. Therefore, it is important for the chief decision makers to consistently establish the tone and tenor for the entire institution. If cultural privilege goes unchecked then it eventually becomes institutionalized in the policies and procedures of universities and other institutions.

Diversity and inclusion matter and helps to bolster the fabric and potency communities. Universities can work with civil rights groups and community organizations to solve seemingly insurmountable problems. It is imperative that the civil rights and higher education communities rally around key areas of convergence and shared values to expand public support for important issues that are paramount to the future of educational and economic opportunity for communities that desperately need it.

North Star Dimensions: The Douglass/Tubman Approach to Social Justice and Inclusion in Higher Education

The version of the North Star that is the brightest star in the constellation was what Harriet Tubman used to guide herself and many others to freedom during the late 1840s and 1850s. The North Star publication, which was the first newspaper that Frederick Douglass founded in 1847, was used as a vehicle to help create the climate for an acceleration of the abolitionist movement, the Civil War, and the eventual ending of chattel slavery in the United States.

Both Tubman and Douglass were pushing the country to be congruent with the ideals that were put forth on the nation's founding documents. They both had a desire for a greater number of people to be included in the opportunities that

America contained and for justice to be spread to those who had too long been denied it. They faced the challenge of contending with a brutal institution of slavery that had existed for nearly two and a half centuries in ways that were different but connected by goals that could appropriately be framed as social justice and inclusion.

The "Tubman dimension" that focuses on individual liberation and the "Douglass dimension" that keys in on collective emancipation are both needed. Communities and students may not be dealing with explicit bondage or captivity in the form of slavery, but there are other chains that need to be broken for everyone to have an equitable shot at living out their potential and for there to be collective community upliftment and individual advancement from a socioeconomic perspective.

Colleges and universities can play a meaningful role in helping people to break out of a limited environment and mindset. There are boundaries that they may have put on themselves and/ or societal restrictions that may have been imposed on them. The fight for social justice and inclusion is a multidimensional process that requires patience, pressure, and persistence.

The Douglass dimension greatly involves identifying various means to create a climate where policy prescriptions can move forward, and systemic change can take place. Douglass used his pen and voice to dramatize the inhuman conditions of slavery through his autobiographies, speaking engagements, and frequent commentary in publications like the North Star. Problems must first be exposed and highlighted before they are addressed in a significant way.

Addressing these problems often involves some kind of confrontation if any substantive deviation from the status quo is going to occur. This may involve the creation of new policies or making intentional efforts to include underrepresented populations in existing programs and practices. Just like with medical prescriptions, policy prescriptions must be consistently applied for a period of time in order for the unwanted symptoms to subside and meaningful change to occur.

The Douglass dimensions raises and follow up on issues like the inclusion of certain populations of students in the "top of line" or "mainstream" opportunities or are there groups who are being systematically relegated to the "chitlin circuit" of lower tier opportunities. For context, chitlins or pig intestines, were among the undesired parts of the hog that slave masters gave to slaves while the owners kept the portions of what was considered to be "high on the hog" like bacon and ham to themselves.

The "chitlin circuit" is what developed during Jim Crowe as a way for Black entertainers to showcase their talents to segregated Black audiences. On the one hand, the "chitlin circuit" provided for a greater level of autonomy within the Black world with Black-owned businesses owning and controlling what was produced from the circuit, but they were also locked out of larger opportunities for economic and social growth and development for generations.

There are systemic trends of inequity that may be progressing without conscious intent but need to be addressed. Some colleges and universities have inadvertently developed a multi-tiered system for the disbursement and allocation of opportunities and resources based on race, ethnicity, gender, religion, disability, and sexual orientation. These are issues that can be brought to the forefront utilizing the Douglass dimension.

This approach brings a social justice and inclusion lens into an institution's policymaking process and employs different tactics to get and keep important issues on the agenda. It facilitates activities that help to create a climate for equity and access to flourish.

The "Tubman dimension" involves finding pathways to help students get the support that they need to fulfill their aspirations and promise. This is the core of what many higher education student service efforts are geared towards. Pathways to personal freedom like Tubman created are also needed for students who need specified supports to navigate to their desired educational and career destinations.

There are many students who are trying to find ways to improve their circumstances and need support. They need "North Star" like services that they can look to for intentional guidance and connection to opportunities that can help them along their journey. If educational institutions are the "North Star", then students can be better able to fulfill their promise. This also includes identifying gatekeeper points that traditionally block student progression and focusing services and supports there.

It is important to note that Tubman did not just show the additional people who were enslaved that she led to freedom the way, but she went with them. She was there every step of the way to monitor their progress and provide the needed information, inspiration, and navigation for them to complete their journeys on the Underground Railroad. In similar fashion, institutions can put people in place to be with students on their journeys and align the appropriate supports to meet students at their needs.

Tubman was not the creator of the underground railroad, but

she executed her role as a conductor at an extremely elite level. The Tubman dimension of social justice and inclusion in higher education centers around the implementation of broader strategies for freedom, development, and empowerment. Implementation at a high level requires grit, determination, consistency, courage, and dedication and is essential to policy being delivered to its intended targets.

The Tubman dimension underscores the importance of following through on proclamations, promises, and policies that may have been passed or agreed upon but have not been fully carried out. A lack of follow up and dedicated efforts to implement initiatives and policies can result in people getting short-changed and slighted over the long run. A system can be put in place, but it cannot be implemented with fidelity without an adequate level of corresponding financial and human resources. The need to continue to organize around and support the people and entities that are charged with delivering policy to the people is critical.

The process of helping students through the Tubman dimension connects to the Douglass dimension in that by helping individual students one can discover trends that can inform and expand efforts that have proven to be effective and impactful. An individual's need for direct support can be highlighted and put forth as a representative example for a broader population. Broader policy can then institutionalize and sustain good efforts and programming.

Ultimately, both dimensions work in unison because systemic changes are necessary as are pathways that empower students to navigate through doors of opportunity. Tubman and Douglass both put their imagination into action as they endeavored to push towards liberation against significant odds. Tubman believed that she could find her way to freedom and go back to free others while rewards for her capture were ever-present, and the journeys grew more and more dangerous. She continued to risk her freedom to free others. Douglass had the audacious belief that he could utilize his God-given gifts of speaking and writing to play a major role in changing a system of slavery that had been in place for over 240 years.

The future of social justice and inclusion in higher education does not have to be locked into old traditions or the ways that it has been in the past. There is room for those who have the foresight to envision new systems and pathways for students and communities and believe that it can be done. The dimensions of the North Star that Douglass and Tubman used to move the nation forward in the areas of social justice and inclusion are still available to institutions of higher education as they continue to serve as arguably the nation's most formidable vehicle of social mobility.

The Pickens Playbook: 7 College Readiness Moves to Make for Student Success

Miami Northwestern Senior High is a school that is nationally known for producing some of the best football players and football teams in the country on a yearly basis. In 2021, the school produced one of the best all-around scholars in the country in George Pickens. He is not only the top ranked academic student in the school, but he is also actively involved in extra-curricular leadership roles.

There is an old adage that says, "success leaves clues". The tremendous academic success of George Pickens has left enough clues to formulate a playbook for others to follow.

George's playbook is special because he has been able to execute in an environment that places an extreme value on young Black males' ability to perform on the football field, but not nearly as much in their ability to excel in other areas. Listed below are seven college readiness plays that George has implemented and are potentially scalable for broader populations of students:

1. Students should set goals and review them on a daily basis.

George said that the first thing that he does when he wakes up in the morning is look at his goals and a vision board that he has made. He looks at both his short-term goals and his long-term goals. This allows him to visualize what he wants to achieve and increases the belief in his ability bring it into fruition.

Guiding and even requiring students formulate and review their goals will increase their focus and help them to see how their daily coursework connects to their broader aspirations. Training students to begin their days by looking within and making investments in their internal development is sure to pay dividends in the form of building the mental and spiritual strength to help them to overcome adversity and to persist in spite of challenges.

2. The elevation of academic achievement is key.

People generally do more and try harder in those areas where they are celebrated and valued. George recalled being celebrated at an end of year ceremony at his elementary school for being the top student in his grade. This encouragement helped to motivate him to continue to achieve at a high level.

The highlighting of academic excellence and the rewards of scholastic success should be put in the forefront with the same enthusiasm that achievement in sports is promoted. Kids growing up in Miami's urban neighborhoods have seen young men go from their same schools and circumstances and achieve National Football League (NFL) fame, fortune, and stardom.

They have seen institutions like the University of Miami and University of Florida come into schools like Miami Northwestern Senior High School and see value in Black boys' ability to play football. These young men are recruited, pursued, and offered full scholarships. The dream for them is real and it seems very attainable. They see and know many examples of it. The same can be done for other routes.

3. Academic competition can generate elite performance.

George competed in math competitions and spelling bees through his involvement in the National Achievers Society since he was in the 6th grade. Group academic competitions like these were a key component to George's success that may differ from a lot of the traditional experiences of the masses of students. The process of training for these competitions with other students allowed for George and others to have the opportunity to both challenge and encourage each other similar to the way that members of a basketball or football team do. Peers push each other to heights that they may not have gotten to if they just trained by themselves.

An aspiring basketball player can do all the drills in the world by himself but he or she will never reach their full potential until they sharpen their craft against competitors that force them to make adjustments and tap into their creativity to get past opposition. The same is true for elite level academic achievement. The Saturday academic practices and competitions were a key factor in George's scholastic acceleration, and they can be for others if more opportunities, venues, and infrastructures are made available.

Competition and celebration should be built around gatekeeper skillsets like math and crucial courses like Algebra. There is rightfully a great emphasis on science, technology, engineering, and mathematics (S.T.E.M.) careers, but S.T.E.M. will become STOP if students don't have the proficiency to pass high level math classes.

Mechanisms that incentivize students to practice math like they practice basketball jump shots and football route running are needed. This play from the Pickens playbook is sure to pay off in the long run with more students being able to take advantage of opportunities in lucrative S.T.E.M. career fields.

4. Participation in sports can be a great developmental tool.

George played football in elementary and middle school for the Miami Gardens Ravens and recalls having fun with his friends. He described football as something that he always loved and was able to connect with. He has been able to translate many of the lessons that he learned on the football field into the classroom like the importance of working hard and consistently practicing in order to produce winning results.

Though George enjoyed playing football, he never bought into the narrative that is dominant in the lives of so many young men that "football is their only way out." He resisted that characterization and didn't see himself as being one dimensional. He maintained a more holistic definition of himself and embraced other leadership roles in extracurricular activities like being the President of the 5000 Role Models of Excellence Project Chapter at his school and the President of the South Florida National Achievers Society.

5. Dual Enrollment = Double Achievement

George began taking dual enrollment classes during the second semester of his freshman year with the goal of graduating with both a high school diploma and an Associate in Arts (AA) degree at the same time. He credits a member of his school's staff for making him aware of the dual enrollment option. The awareness of the availability of this opportunity was crucial as many students miss out on opportunities like dual enrollment because they are not provided information about it in a timely manner.

George's decision to take advantage of the dual enrollment opportunities that were made available to him through his high school and Miami Dade College were key to building additional momentum to keep him going. This momentum helped him to maximize his days and maintain the grueling daily regimen that this double duty required. He would find periods during the day to do the necessary assignments and classwork. These time slots would be during breaks in classes, during lunch, commuting, and late at night when he got home from the Miami Dade College North Campus.

He was keenly aware that graduating with his high school diploma and AA degree simultaneously would give him a strong foundation and lay the groundwork for what he wanted to achieve in his life and the kind of impact that he wanted to make. This kind of awareness can build one's focus and push them to maintain the kind of habits and regimen that George was able to implement.

6. Career exploration helps to generate a sense of purpose.

George found a sense of purpose early in his life in seeing the issues that persisted in his community like gun violence and unequal access to healthcare. It motivated him to want to be a part of the solution by becoming a medical doctor and social advocate. He considers himself to be a service-oriented person and relishes opportunities to lend a helping hand.

The medical magnet program at Northwestern was a part of his attraction to the school. The program introduces students to various careers in the medical field as early as the 9th grade and they are also able to get industry certifications. Some of the teachers who teach the courses in the magnet program are also medical professionals, so they get instruction from those who are currently working in the field.

The importance of cultivating future healthcare professionals like George who value the treating of patients with care, compassion, and humanity is vital. The COVID-19 pandemic and the restrictions around the family visitation of patients who are in the hospital has heightened the significance of how hospital personnel interact with patients. Hospital staff are now the only people in many cases that patients interact with and they are dependent on them for company, motivation, and care while they are dealing with their affliction.

7. Mentorship and examples to emulate are critical.

One of the key infrastructures of opportunity that has benefitted George and thousands of others in Miami-Dade County is the 5000 Role Models of Excellence Project, a dropout prevention and mentorship program founded by U.S. Congresswoman Frederica Wilson in 1993. The program has chapters of boys in 110 schools in the county who receive mentorship, life skills training, and exposure to a myriad of different experiences from health summits to prison visits to college tours to trips to Washington D.C. and more.

George joined the 5000 Role Models when he was in the 5th grade and has been a part of chapters at his elementary, middle, and high school. He became the President of the 5000 Role Models chapter at Miami Northwestern Senior High School. One of the most impactful experiences for George was a trip to a local prison where he came face to face with the realities of the mass incarceration epidemic and where the consequences of a bad decision or even being at the wrong place at the wrong time could lead him.

George appreciates the way that being a 5000 Role Model has helped to shape his character. It embodies brotherhood for him and has exposed him to various issues and careers within his community that he may have otherwise overlooked. Though the program, he has been able to have numerous speaking opportunities including him introducing President Barack Obama at a Miami rally in October of 2020.

The brotherhood and positive peer pressure that is generated from programs like the 5000 Role Models has had an incalculable impact on the development of young men and should be institutionalized in school districts across the nation.

The development of life skills, character building, and quality decision making are key factors that George acquired from other sources in addition to the 5000 Role Models. The primary source was his family. His late mother was an educator, and his father is a professional in the engineering field. They both emphasized the importance of education and the doors that it could open for him. His older sister was a stellar scholar and set a great example for him to follow and emulate.

This kind of family set up may not be replicable for the broader population of students, but there are other resources and infrastructures like the 5000 Role Models of Excellence Project that can be put in place to provide a consistent level of positive nurturing and support.

These seven plays from Pickens College Readiness Playbook can be adopted by other students and by systems and structures that are geared toward student development. It is important to note that this playbook does not guarantee success. It will not automatically give one the many intangible factors that George possesses and has consistently employed like grit, determination, focus, discipline, and the ability to delay gratification, but it can serve as a starting point for transformational change.

The playbook for athletic excellence has been instilled, replicated, and institutionalized in the hearts and minds of young men of color and the communities that they inhabit. Playbooks for academic excellence can be embedded in the same way. Success is not guaranteed, but the combination of the right plays and the will to execute them are a formidable force to contend with. It is time to take a new look at what is working in our communities and schools and find innovative ways to scale them to broader populations of students so that they can be better prepared for access and success at higher education institutions.

The Pickens Playbook Part 2: Year One at Tennessee State University

It was the final week of April 2021, and the clock was running out for Miami Northwestern Senior High School Senior George Pickens to make his final decision on where he would be going to pursue higher education. Pickens, who graduated as the top ranked student in his senior class, was the subject of a previous section entitled "The Pickens Playbook: 7 College Readiness Moves to Make for Student Success".

Pickens had many different choices including Harvard University, Howard University, Duke University, and the University of Miami. Ultimately, he felt that he could not turn down the opportunity to go into the Bachelor of Science/ Doctor of Medicine (BS/MD) Program at Tennessee State University (TSU) which included acceptance into the Meharry Medical College School of Medicine upon completion of his undergraduate work at TSU.

He was also impressed by the outreach and genuine efforts of the TSU administration following his visit to the campus in early April 2021. On his visit, he met with program staff and was given a personalized campus tour with Mr. and Ms. TSU. After he returned to Miami, personnel from the program called him every day to check up on him and give him guidance and support leading up to the May 1st decision deadline. He remarked that their persistence showed him how much they cared for students.

Pickens and his fellow cohort members of the Dr. Levi Watkins Jr. Accelerated Pathway Program (BS/MD students) arrived on campus in late July, a few weeks before other students. They went to Meharry Medical College every day and heard testimonials from doctors and students. He described it as a two-week period of building connections and solidifying a long-term support system there. He also got a chance to build camaraderie with other members of his cohort.

After the orientation period, George was selected by an external organization, Baxter International, to receive scholarship support that would cover his enrollment through the completion of his medical school tenure after he matriculates to Meharry Medical College. These experiences helped to lay a solid foundation for an academic year that would end with him enjoying a great academic and social life balance on the TSU campus and finishing the academic year with a 4.0 grade point average. Below are some plays from the "Pickens Playbook" that helped him continue to build on his positive academic momentum at the collegiate level.

Remember why you came to college and remind yourself every day.

Pickens begins every day thinking about where he started and where he wants to go. He believes that this helps him to align with his mission and reconnects him to his faith. He stated that "I keep my mind focused on what I believe that a big part of my purpose is to equip myself to be able to assist others on a daily basis and pour back into the community that poured into me. I become truly happy through service."

This mindset gives him the continuous motivation to put forth the consistent time, energy, and focus that is required for him to maintain his stellar grade point average. He challenges himself to be a better version of himself on that day than he was the previous day. He understands that he will have to work for what he wants and who he wants to become. Pickens expressed this by saying that "success comes to those who work for it. It comes to those who wake up an hour earlier and stay up an hour later."

College is what you make of it.

Many students who will be matriculating to institutions of higher education will be experiencing a freedom that they had never previously had. They are essentially on their own to allocate their time and energy in whatever way they would like. It can understandably be difficult for people to be able to handle their newfound autonomy. Those who excel in this environment must be intentional about prioritizing their time and appropriately balancing their academic and social lives.

Every Sunday, Pickens creates a schedule for himself for the upcoming week with what he wants to accomplish and when he intends on doing it. He then tries to stick as closely as he can to that schedule though there are inevitably some things that come up that may cause him to deviate from what was planned. He understands and enjoys the social aspect of college life but has set a rule for himself that he must complete the academic work that he aims to achieve for the day before attending social events. He knows that it can be much more difficult to try to get this kind of work done after a late-night event on campus or somewhere else in the city.

Find a study routine that works for you.

Pickens knew that he would have to retool and redesign the study habits that he had in high school as he was transitioning into a different city, campus, and academic institution. He went through a trial-and-error process to see what worked and what didn't work in terms of maximizing his study time.

He initially tried studying in his room but found it to be not the most conducive to long term concentration with his bed right there and other distractions readily available. He eventually settled on sequestering himself in a room in the library where he would put his phone on "do not disturb" for a few hours and see how much he could accomplish during that period of dedicated focus. He found this to work for him in a way that enabled him to establish a consistent daily routine where he could maximize his productivity during his planned study time.

Understand your place in history.

Pickens has a keen understanding of history and a deep appreciation for those who paved the way for him to have the opportunities that he is currently able to have. TSU, an institution that was founded on June 19, 1912, as the Tennessee Agricultural & Industrial State Normal School for Negroes and has long been a primary access point for students to continue their education and uplift their communities.

110 years after its founding, students like Pickens continue to build onto this legacy and blaze important traits particularly in the field of medicine where the percentage of Black male doctors in 2018 was 2.6%, slightly under the 2.7% of Black male doctors in 1940. The production of more students like Pickens will be key to improving these numbers in the future.

Pickens is already a trailblazer by being the first student in the Class of 2021 from the 5000 Role Models of Excellence Project, a dropout prevention and mentorship program founded by Congresswoman Frederica Wilson, to secure a scholarship offer from TSU and ultimately commit to going. This helped to open the way for 11 other Florida-based students from the program to come in 2021 and an additional 42 students from the Class of 2022 who will be joining the initial cohort this Fall.

The internal drive that Pickens has consistently generated within himself to produce successful outcomes in multiple areas of life is especially commendable. What Pickens has already accomplished has required day after day, week after week, and month after month of disciplined effort with minimal applause or celebration compared to other more celebrated pathways like athletics and entertainment.

His ability to delay gratification and remain focused on his purpose while taking the needed incremental steps of preparation to equip himself for excellence is worthy of study and is a large part of the basis of this evolving "playbook". The key to his external achievement; has been his internal investment in his mental, spiritual, and intellectual development.

These plays from George Pickens include adjustments that students can incorporate to better prioritize their time and energy to have exceptional academic performance and still enjoy the social experience of college.

Connecting Today's Course Activities to Tomorrow's Career Possibilities is Key to Student Re-engagement

To say that education and learning has been significantly disrupted by the COVID-19 pandemic would be an understatement. Students have had to adjust to a new form of being educated while instructors were learning new methods on the fly. It was a patchwork process at best, but it caused a reexamination of existing practices.

Strategies to engage students coming out of the COVID-19 pandemic will need to be updated from those that were employed prior to the pandemic. The World has shifted and all who are involved in the educational space will need to shift also. The virtual learning environment has been advantageous for a highly motivated set of students who have been able to thrive over the past year, but very detrimental to other students who have become disillusioned with their classes and academic work.

This has been the case in both in secondary and post-secondary educational settings. While some students have had a maintained an elevated level of focus, others have been taken off track by distractions like video games, social media, and the bed while learning at home. There are students who found any excuse to not turn their screen on during Zoom or Microsoft Teams course sessions, enabling them to be counted as present on the class roll but absent in the learning experience.

The problem of student disengagement and disinterest in coursework is one that may have significant ramifications well into the future. The need for intentional efforts to reengage students in the learning process is more important now than any other time in the recent past because of the well documented anticipated learning losses (Dickler, 2021).

One way to help students reengage is to emphasize their value. The value that a person puts on themselves dictates a great deal of their decision making. If their sense of self-worth and value is high, then they are more likely to be motivated to apply themselves to their studies and maximize their academic potential. Self-esteem is not something that should be neglected or taken for granted because it ties right into a student's belief that they can do the work.

If one doesn't believe that they can do it then they may not even try. Some students don't engage in their studies in a meaningful way because they have convinced themselves that they won't be successful. There is a belief gap that is preventing progress. Disengagement may be a way of avoiding what they feel will be obvious failure. This is something that can be difficult to turn around, but it can be contended against with consistent encouragement and the highlighting of the valuable attributes that students do possess. Self-esteem and self-value are something that needs to be intentionally cultivated and supported. They are foundational building blocks to greater achievement.

Additionally, supporters can emphasize the relevance of their day-to-day coursework. People don't like to be engaged in exercises of futility for a sustained period. There is a need to draw clear and direct lines to how coursework applies to the "real world". The practice of applying the lesson to life is critical for students who are disengaged and may not see the point of being in a particular class outside of just getting a grade.

Effective instructors can draw direct lines that illuminate clearly how today's activities can connect to tomorrow's possibilities. Taking the time to outline the knowledge, skills, and abilities that will be required to build a bridge from the activity to an economically viable skillset is time well spent. It can certainly be a challenge to convey that what students do now is important for their future in the years to come. It can be hard to make that connection. It's easy to become a prisoner of the moment. A video game can seemingly have more relevance in the moment than an academic class.

Intervening on a consistent basis with different ways that coursework is relevant to students' future and careers is critical to reengage students who may be disconnected from applying themselves to their studies. This is a time to put additional focus on being more purposeful with pedagogy and curriculum. Helping students find a longer-term purpose for their daily coursework is likely to increase attendance, engagement, and performance in scholastic endeavors.

Creating pathways that are connected to student passions and strengths is another way to increase student engagement.

These core elements can be coupled with the development of complementary skillsets that can build the needed momentum to push students to new levels. Instructors can facilitate the exploration of different opportunities with students that are connected to each of their passions. Their passions should become connection hubs for supporters to plug different opportunities and experiences into.

After the connections and correlations are made plain, students can receive guidance on what additional efforts they can make on their own and the appropriate times to make intentional links with resources to help them along their journey. Finding ways to systematically unleash the possibilities that are connected to the activities that students already enjoy has the potential to transform dropout rates and significantly reduce the number of disengaged students.

Harrison Champions Increased Student Access at Miami Dade College

Miami Dade College (MDC) Provost Dr. Malou Harrison has taken aggressive and direct action to address gaps in higher education access and success for Black students through her spearheading of the Rising Black Scholars program. According to a press release from the college the program "will provide Black students graduating from high school in 2021 with free tuition for up to two years of study, creating a coherent academic and career pathway leading to an associate degree and increased earning potential" (Miami Dade College, 2021).

The initiative is an example of how individuals like Dr. Harrison can help to bolster institutional belief in a population of students who have historically been the most underrepresented in higher education institutions. Before opportunity and achievement gaps are closed; the belief gap must be addressed. This involves both the students' belief in their own ability and the institution's belief in the students.

Dr. Harrison's unapologetic effort to open unprecedented doors of opportunity should be applauded. It takes courage to take such a stand and it is a focused initiative that is much needed. It is a move that indicates that Black students are wanted and valued at the institution, and it is in alignment with MDC's continuing efforts to better build a culture that supports them.

This access and outreach effort has the potential to build a better connection among students by cultivating peer bonding and a supportive ecosystem. Belief, care, and support in tandem with the tangible financial benefits of the program form the elements of an initiative that will not just be about a transactional exchange, but rather a transformational experience. The program is designed to go beyond the provision of tuition, books, and a laptop and provide a holistic array of support services that includes opportunities to gain stackable credentials, career exploration guidance, academic advisement, internship opportunities, and resume assistance. These proactive strategies will help to prepare students for post-college success.

The services that accompany the program will be specifically targeted to meet the unique needs of these scholars who have a distinct set of challenges and opportunities. There is power in precision. The late actor Bruce Lee once said that "I fear not that man who has practiced 10,000 kicks once, but I fear the man who has practiced one kick 10,000 times." Specific challenges require specific responses. If this population of students can be lifted, then the entire student body will be lifted.

The bold moves that have been made by Dr. Harrison and supported by the institution are the kind that are needed during this time of unprecedented challenges. It has given students a new opportunity to fulfill their dreams and it can be a launching for other innovative approaches like the expansion of peer-to-peer mentorship, academic enhancement, socioemotional development, and civic engagement.

This core group of scholars can encourage each other and motivate other students to strive for academic success and persist through degree attainment. They will be well positioned to be on the leading edge and prepared to maximize their ability. Partnerships with similarly aligned K-12 programs can form a pipeline that will increase the level of college and career preparation for everyone involved.

The Rising Black Scholars program is not a "cure all" for the underrepresentation of Black students that persists at institutions of higher education, but it is a giant leap forward both from a resource and commitment standpoint. Dr. Harrison should be saluted for using her position power to provide opportunities to a population of students who are too often dismissed and disregarded. A new paradigm of a more equitable playing field is on the horizon at Miami Dade College and other institutions that have launched similar initiatives.

TSU President Dr. Glenda Glover and Congresswoman Frederica Wilson Establish Partnership for Higher Education Access

Alpha Kappa Alpha Sorority Inc. sisters and leaders in their respective arenas Congresswoman Frederica Wilson and Dr. Glenda Glover have structured a groundbreaking partnership that will open the doors of higher education opportunity to students from Miami-Dade, Broward, and Duval Counties in Florida. Glover, President of Tennessee State University (TSU), has awarded full scholarships to more than 50 students from the 5000 Role Models of Excellence Project, a dropout prevention and mentorship program for boys and young men of color that was founded by Wilson in 1993.

This Florida to Nashville higher education pipeline is not new but is one that is being reinvigorated and reinforced with this new effort. Wilson herself went to Nashville to attend Fisk University after graduating from Miami Northwestern Senior High School. TSU is continuing to show that institutions of higher education can be hubs for providing pathways to access post-secondary educational instruction, connect students with emerging economic opportunities, and inspire them to fulfill their purpose. The university is rapidly asserting itself not just as a bedrock institution for students within the state of Tennessee but also as a national academic destination as it has been in years past for those who want to gain the training to maximize their potential.

This partnership also continues to expand on the 5000 Role Models of Excellence Project's mission to disrupt the school-to-prison pipeline by creating new pathways of opportunity through higher education. This group of 5000 Role Model students includes the valedictorian of Miami Northwestern Senior High School, George Pickens IV, who chose TSU over the University of Miami, Howard University, Duke University, and Harvard University among others. Pickens is a part of an initiative that targets future Black male doctors in a joint arrangement with Meharry Medical College.

Pickens reflected on his decision to go to TSU by saying "I didn't choose TSU, instead TSU chose me. When making my college decision, I consulted mentors, family, friends, and of course prayed about it. At first it seemed as if the signs were small and I often overlooked them, but as time progressed it became evident that TSU was the best fit for me. I am excited to further my education at a school that stands for service and excellence and is deeply rooted in history."

Another member of the group, Rodga Laurius from Miami Edison Senior High School, grew up in Miami's Little Haiti neighborhood and is relishing the opportunity to go into a new environment with the opportunity to pursue a higher education. Laurius received a call in April 2021 about the opportunity to go to TSU and was shocked. He said that he was "thrilled and excited to have this life changing opportunity. I get a chance to go to school outside of the state and meet new people and have new experiences."

The continuation and extension of infrastructures of opportunity like the 5000 Role Models of Excellence Project is an important step towards reducing the number of disconnected youth. Disconnected youth are those individuals between 18 and 24 that are neither working or in school. An overabundance of this disconnected population translates into a massive amount of wasted potential. This underutilized talent is laid to waste in large part because students don't receive enough direction and affirmation to see it through to its full development.

An increased level of intentionality is needed to ensure that support for young people does not cease after they leave high school. Strong transfers from one support system to another must take place to prevent students from falling through the cracks. One system of institutional support does not have to totally replace another but can build upon and compliment the previous one. The positionality of support systems for these students may change with TSU in this example becoming the primary one, but the 5000 Role Models of Excellence Project is set up to continue to be active and impactful in the lives of the students who are matriculating to TSU.

The explosion of virtual meeting spaces like Zoom and Microsoft Teams enables continued connectivity despite groups of people not being in the same physical location. Cohorts like this group of students who are headed to TSU can connect with other cohorts who may be engaging in similar processes in other parts of the country. As institutions of higher education prepare to pivot back to a predominately in-person learning environment, elements of the virtual educational experience that was accelerated during the COVID-19 pandemic can be carried forward to create an even more robust scholastic program.

These kinds of institutional partnerships can help to turn needed corners into greater avenues of progress that may have been previously blocked by external or internal barriers. TSU President Dr. Glenda Glover and Congresswoman Frederica Wilson have delivered big for these students, and it is a great example for other institutions and organizations to follow.

Commission on the Social Status of Black Men and Boys Can Be a Railroad for Best Practices

As the country approaches another anniversary of the killing of George Floyd by Minneapolis, Minnesota Police Officer Derek Chauvin, questions about where the movement for social justice will go from here continue to abound. Legislative progress in directly addressing the plight of Black men like Floyd has been an uphill battle. The George Floyd Justice in Policing Act has been passed by the U.S. House of Representatives but has not yet been voted on in the Senate.

The primary piece of national legislation that was passed as a direct response to Floyd's killing was a bill that established the Commission on the Social Status of Black Men and Boys. The legislation was introduced in the House by Democratic Congresswoman Frederica Wilson and in the Senate by Republican Senator Marco Rubio. It was passed by both houses of Congress in July of 2020 and was signed into law by former President Donald Trump in August of 2020.

According to a press release from Congresswoman Wilson's office, the bill "establishes a permanent, bipartisan commission within the United States Commission on Civil Rights. Its 19 members will include congressional lawmakers, executive branch appointees, issue experts, activists, and other stakeholders who will examine social disparities affecting black men and boys in America. Based on its findings, the commission will issue policy recommendations to Congress, the White House, and federal agencies" (Congressional Black Caucus, 2020).

This Commission will elevate issues like disparities in "education, criminal justice, health, employment, fatherhood, mentorship, and violence" and create an infrastructure to press toward the goal of better understanding and eventually eliminating the conditions that have made it extraordinarily difficult for an unacceptably high number of black males to become upwardly mobile.

The implications of the Commission for higher education may be manifold. One potential way that it could be utilized is as a "railroad" to carry best practices for access, retention, and completion for Black males in higher education to institutions across the country. The Commission presents a new opportunity to examine what is working and fortify those practices, programs, and procedures with resources to incentive the expansion of these infrastructures of opportunity.

There may not be one template that works everywhere, but there are sets of common practices and principles that have shown patterns of sustained success and scalability that can be molded to fit the needs of different localities and institutions. The Commission can complement and help to expand existing efforts and build the capacity of those who are already engaging in the space. A coordinated and concentrated effort like this with the backing of multiple federal departments and stakeholders can push through barriers that typically prevent needed expansions of successful systems.

Higher education institutions can be the linchpin of these efforts because of their ability to provide multiple connection points for both Black men and boys. Higher education is still the most accessible ladder out of poverty. Colleges, universities, and trade schools should be partners with the work of the Commission. They are a direct feeder for boys that are exiting high school, a hub for the upskilling of men to become or remain economically relevant, and a potential partner for K-12 schools and community organizations that serve every age group of boys and men.

The "railroads" that can be created by the Commission can carry the nation's best practices to post-secondary educational institutions to help deploy them for the usage of the broader community. They can serve as distribution centers to pump opportunity into underserved communities. There is a higher education point of connectivity to every aspect of the

Commission's aim and charge including addressing joblessness, health disparities, academic achievement gaps, and disparate treatment in the criminal justice system.

Legislative proposals that are generated from the Commission can incentivize with significant funding those practices that can directly address the systematic targeting of Black men and boys for destruction. They are being hit with a duplicitous combination of an overhand right jab of mass incarceration and a lethal left hook of economic marginalization. This combination has served in many cases to lock out and lock up a disproportionate number of Black men. The Commission is one of the only federal forms of recourse that this population has and can be a mighty weapon against systems that have caused great harm to the quality of life of the Black community at large.

The formation of this embedded federal effort can fight back against these challenges with education, mentorship, access to capital, and policies and practices that will provide solutions and redress for an accrued disadvantage that has resulted from slavery, Jim Crowe, redlining, discrimination in employment and contacts, harsher penalties for the same infractions, mass incarceration and the list goes on and on.

The bottom line is that there are systems and institutions that have consistently produced racial disparate outcomes regardless of the intentions of the people who work within them. The lack of overt or deliberate racism sometimes masks an unintentional bias that is embedded in many policies. Systemic racism neither begins nor ends with police brutality. The opportunity chasms for Black men and boys that are glaringly apparent in the data are often the cumulative effect of subtle and silent moves that are made behind closed doors that lock them out of pivotal opportunities. A series of systematic attacks requires a series of systematic responses.

As the country moves back towards "normalcy" after the COVID-19 pandemic has gripped the country for an extended period of time, we should be reminded that the status quo did not work well for the masses of Black men and boys. We should be reminded that normalcy has meant exclusion and looking at disparity and shrugging. Higher education institutions can seize this moment and help the Commission leverage their power in a strategic and courageous way to transform and reorganize the nation's institutions to advance the plight of Black males and the country at large.

This unprecedented federal apparatus with a direct focus on Black men and boys can be a railroad that carries prosperity and progress to a population that has faced enormous barriers and challenges. Change is not always about the creation of new legislation, but it can also be about maximizing the potential of the current policies that are already on the books. The Commission on the Social Status of Black Men and Boys can help the nation can surge ahead with what is already there while still striving for new legislative advancements.

A Revolution in Teacher Pay is Needed to Recruit and Retain the Best and Brightest

Numerous studies including Goldhaber (2016) have shown that the key factor that impacts student academic performance the most is the quality of the teacher that is in the classroom. It would therefore make logical sense to place significant financial investment into recruiting and producing teachers of the highest quality if the goal is to improve student performance.

The higher the quality of the teacher, the better the education that students will receive. There must be a significant increase in the renumeration of those who are investing in the students on a regular basis.

The battle for the future of education begins with motivating the best college and university students to choose to pursue careers in education. It is extremely difficult to do that with the existing non-competitive salaries and limited career trajectory structures that permeate educational systems. Advancements in curriculum, pedagogy, and school management strategies should be accompanied by financial incentives that are on par with other industries to lure top level talent.

The priority must be to allure and attract the best possible potential educators to teach and pour into the next generations. Unfortunately, many people who would be phenomenal teachers can't financially afford to be teachers. Too many of the best and brightest higher education students in terms of academic performance won't even consider careers in education because the salaries won't allow them to live comfortably in many areas.

The missing link is investing in the link between students and the education that they receive. You can't have an impoverished system of inputs and reasonably expect an abundant production of outputs. You can't bypass producers if you want consistent production. Sometimes reform needed and sometimes revolution is required. It is time for a revolution in teacher pay beginning with a minimum starting salary of $80,000 across the board.

The existing teacher workforce should not be overlooked in the effort to recruit great new teachers. Teachers who are currently working in classrooms have stabilized the existing implementation of educational programming and deserve to have a level a financial stability that allows them to lock in even more on perfecting their craft. Their economic status should be lifted at a rate that is proportionately above the rate the new teachers that need to be attracted to the profession.

Unfortunately, many teachers can barely afford the necessities of life in a lot of major cities. The salaries of teachers have not even come close to keeping up with the rising cost of living. Economic stability needs to be provided to those who are pouring into children daily. Even those who may have a supreme calling to the teaching profession eventually realize the reality of escalating bills and other financial obligations.

Too many great teachers are forced to leave the profession because they find it too difficult to make ends meet. Temporary raises or episodic bonuses will not be sufficient in the long run. There needs to be dedicated funding streams that revolutionize the status and appeal of the teaching profession. Teachers deserve to be respected and have a competitive salary.

The challenge of the recruitment and retainment of high-quality teachers is perhaps the most important one for the future of education. The education of children deserves to be a vocation that is intentionally chosen and not one that people just fall into by default. That will not happen without tremendous increases in teacher pay. The best and brightest educators need to be incentivized to deliver high level curriculum and programming to students. Adequately funding education means more than just providing facilities and supplies. It is time for a revolution of financial investment in teachers who are the crucial link between students and the high-quality education that they deserve.

A Lack of Bread to Win is Why There Aren't More Black Male Teachers

Why aren't there more Black male teachers? I recently attended a forum where this question was posed. I contend that a lack of intergenerational wealth transfers due to the historic exclusion of Blacks from many wealth building opportunities is a primary reason why there aren't more Black male teachers. This along with the societal expectations of men needing to be the "breadwinners" for families deter many men from desiring to go into areas where there is a perceived lack of bread to win.

Unless one has a substantial intergenerational wealth transfer like someone gifting them with housing, a down payment, inheritance, investments, or money that is in addition to their own earned income then it is extremely difficult in most major metro areas to financially support a family on a teacher's salary.

Black males are simply starting from too far behind on average economically to move en masse into a subpar paying sector when they must compete in the marketplace for goods and services with their earnings garnered in one lifetime versus others who are much more likely to have multiple lifetimes of wealth funneled to them through higher levels of intergenerational wealth transfers that bolster their financial resources.

Until there is a major change in the perception and reality of teacher compensation then I do not believe that there will be any significant movement in the number of Black male teachers. Efforts to recruit retired military personnel, police officers, and others who have a second form of passive income in the form of a pension or other source may be a viable strategy to help address immediate teacher shortages while many governments are still unwilling to drastically revolutionize teacher pay in a way that would make it competitive with higher wage industries.

Even those who have a tremendous passion for teaching may be forced to leave the profession to simply maintain a minimal standard of living amidst rapidly escalating inflation and housing prices.

Americans must face the choice of continuing to treat the teacher workforce as a charitable mission or shift to making it into an economically competitive industry that the best and brightest of our students' desire to go into with intentionality as opposed to a default fall back up plan to go into if nothing else works out as is too often the case. How do we get more Black male teachers? Increase the amount of bread to win in the profession.

PART 4: BRIGHTER WAYS FORWARD

The unpacking of brighter ways forward will be a combination of highlighting some policies, practices, and programs that deserve to be scaled in some way, providing insight into strategic partnerships that would likely accelerate progress in different areas. There is also a sizable portion of this part that deals with the mental, spiritual, and emotional development of individuals. There is an emphasis on this because communities are made up of individuals and as people become better holistic versions of themselves, communities will be uplifted in turn.

The internal aspects that lead to higher levels of economic and emotional viability like faith, self-esteem, internal validation, overcoming adversity, and courageously living in one's purpose are explored in part four.

A Brighter Way: Winning the Battle Between Blight Hustling and Bright Hustling

Certain conditions in life can lead many of us with no choice but to hustle. There is a "do or die" mentality that goes along with being in a circumstance where there is either no safety net or a limited one. There can be a sense of desperation that can either lead to a series of increasingly detrimental decisions or it can generate a supreme level of focus and dedication that drives one to levels of achievement beyond what they could previously comprehend. In one way or another, hustling is what ultimately lifts one out of extreme circumstances to a better way of life.

Hustle, defined by dictionary.com as a verb meaning "to proceed or work rapidly or energetically", is often a key factor in social mobility for individual people and broader communities. Hustling is a foundational element of American culture and society and is a multidimensional concept. A battle is being waged in many schools and communities over which aspect of "hustling" will become culturally dominant and guide the focus of students and prospective students.

Dr. Michael Eric Dyson provided descriptions for bright hustling and blight hustling in his book "JAY-Z: Made in America". Dyson described blight hustling as something that happens on the street corners of American society. Those who have their backs against the wall and feel that they are forced to go into the underground economy and cooperate with ill-gotten gain (Dyson & Williams, 2019).

Dyson wrote that "positive, legitimate, legal hustling can be termed bright hustling. It encompasses a wide range of activities: creating multiple streams of income, renting a room in your house, earning passive income through real estate investments, opening a small business, building banks, donating blood for money, coming up with a computer software app for mobile devices, getting a Ph.D., playing professional sports, becoming a lawyer, doctor, engineer, hairdresser, barber....."

This choice between blight hustling and bright hustling is one that many adults, both young and old, are having to contend with as additional governmental supports associated with the

COVID-19 pandemic continue to subside. The pressure to hustle gets ratcheted up as the weight of economic needs and expectations continue to build.

The pull and temptation to engage in blight hustling increases as bright hustling avenues appear dim. The immediate need for resources and gratification that blight hustling can appear to satisfy is a mighty one to contend with. Additionally, blight hustling is often mass marketed and glorified through music, television, and movies. It is hard to do long-term thinking and cultivate the ability to delay gratification when you are trying to figure out what and how you are going to eat that night.

For adults, figuring out how you are going to pay bills when there is more month than money often trumps theoretical concepts and vague policy proposals. The more extreme situations become, the blurrier the lines between good and bad and ethical and non-ethical become. The cost of housing, gas, food, and other elements that make up one's quality of life are quickly accelerating while wages are either stagnating or only slightly improving. This increases the pressure on both younger and older students who are dealing with deciding between bright and blight hustling scenarios.

Higher education institutions would be prudent to adapt their programming and the way that they present their offerings to make the benefits of bright hustling more appealing than the potential spoils of blight hustling. It is not enough to condemn blight hustling without providing ways where economic sustenance can be met with bright hustling. Tangible impact on one's day-to-day quality of life should be highlighted and fortified with legitimate opportunities for economic and social mobility.

There is a premium on high quality programs that can give students the credentials and skills that they need in a relatively short period of time. This means going beyond just putting something in place to say that you have something, but it requires going the extra mile to examine the quality of the program and to make sure that the credentials that students receive are connected to higher tier employment and economic opportunities.

One idea is to make a massive investment in providing paid experiential learning opportunities to people where they can get paid to work in areas that will provide them with the tools for longer term economic viability and money to support their immediate financial needs. Additionally, the expansion of access and funding for shorter training programs that produce sought after certifications in data analytics, Kubernetes, and supply chain logistics could also have appeal to students who are looking to make transformational career moves.

There is choice and agency even within the midst of adverse circumstances. People need to have choices that lead to their empowerment and support through every step of their higher education process. The communication channels and messengers that are selected to deliver post-secondary educational options to prospective students are pivotal. The more credible and trusted the source of information is in the eyes of the intended target, the more likely it is that the information will be acted on in a meaningful way.

Brighter ways to get to one's desired destination can be uncovered and pursued, but it must be understood that they will have to compete to win against blight-oriented alternatives. These battles take place and are won in "the trenches" and not in "ivory towers". It is time for higher education officials to roll up their sleeves and do some bright hustling for a better future.

The Transferrable Impact of Positive Pressure in Sports and Public Policy

Pressure is something that people may tend to resist. It can make a person uncomfortable. It can push one into an environment that contains a heightened level of stress. It often involves a confrontation of some sort that forces a decision or a certain course of action within a defined time. There are lessons in applying and handling pressure in sports and efforts to change public policy that can be garnered and transferred to other areas like higher education teaching, learning, research, and service.

President Franklin D. Roosevelt is known for saying "okay, you've convinced me. Now get out there and bring pressure on me." Roosevelt was affirmatively welcoming the pressure that was ultimately going to be needed to bring about necessary change. He was opening his arms to pressure. The key to operating well under pressure is to embrace it and not resist it; to run towards it and not away from it. If used the right way, pressure can be a blessing and not a burden. Exposure to pressure builds up one's tolerance to operate with excellence under adverse circumstances.

The buildup of pressure on the government in Cuba in 2021 is what protestors have brought upon their ruling regime and what their allies in the United States are trying to sustain. They are attempting to exert pressure on any forces who may be able to impact the existing arrangement that has marginalized people in Cuba for decades. Their aim is to ultimately put so much pressure on the status quo in Cuba that the current course of action is untenable. The Cuban protestors have indicated a desire to not be confined to the status quo.

Pressure is often accompanied by a sense of urgency. The urgency is what makes the status quo unacceptable and what forces action. Crises, be they intentional or unintentional, bring different forms of pressure with them. There is both individual and societal pressure that people, communities, states, and nations feel. Pressure can cause people or entities to take action that they would not have taken or were opposed to, and it can cause people to act on things that they wanted to do or at least were not in opposition to sooner.

Pressure is also one the key elements that is needed to produce winning sports teams and standout athletes on a consistent basis. It has been applied to achieve athletic excellence for generations and the same principles can be applied to other areas. One example is college and university sports coaches who excel at a high level. They are amongst those who are the most vested in the development and maximization of the ability of their student-athletes. They have literally "bet the house" on it. Their livelihood directly depends on the performance of their players.

One take away from this that is transferrable to other areas is that there often must be some level of personal investment or something personal on the line for people to maximize anything. People can deal with and even embrace an increased level of pressure if they feel that the payoff is worth it. The amount of pressure and payoff must be raised at an equivalent level for people to stay optimally engaged in their chosen profession over the long haul.

This is one of the factors that has prompted many coaches to turn over almost every stone they can and look for different strategies to develop the talent of individual players, devise a multitude of plays for the team to work together to overcome opposing schemes, and look at every detail they can that can potentially impact whether their team wins or loses.

There is a heightened level of immersion and focus that goes into what coaches do every day because the stakes are higher. With higher stakes comes more pressure. Pressure one of the main elements that leads to top level performance on a consistent basis. A lack of pressure leads to complacency which is the enemy of the maximization of one's potential and purpose.

The application of pressure can be seen around us every day in different ways. Deadlines, standards, expectations, and certain traditions are all ways of applying pressure. Time is a key component to pressure. The more urgent the time restraint or deadline is or seems the more pressure is felt by those who are impacted. This the why the seventh game of a seven-game series in sports has more inherent pressure than the first or second game. The series is over after game seven. Time has expired. The element of a deadline brings with it a "do or die" mentality. Something must be done, a decision must be made, and a definite action must be taken. Sitting on the fence or continuing to take no action is no longer an option.

Pressure has also been utilized by historic leaders of the past to bring about changes in public policy. Historic leaders Frederick Douglass, A. Philip Randolph, and Dr. Martin Luther King Jr. utilized pressure to help create the momentum for significant policy changes.

Douglass recognized the need for a national confrontation

to occur for slavery to ultimately be ended. He generated pressure on the status quo prior to the Civil War through his speeches across the country and his writing. He continued to hammer down on how unacceptable slavery was and on how military intervention was necessary. This helped to create an environment of a heightened level of pressure.

During the Civil War, he pressured President Abraham Lincoln on both making the ending of slavery one of the primary goals of the war and on permitting Black soldiers to fight in the war. Douglass would recruit Black soldiers including two of his own sons to fight which ultimately helped to turn the tide of the war leading to a Union victory and the emancipation of the slaves. Without this pressure, Lincoln could have potentially ended the war without freeing the slaves which was his stated intent as late as 1862 (Lincoln, 1862). His initial goal was focused primarily on preserving the Union. Positive pressure prevailed.

Randolph and other civil rights leaders used pressure to push President Franklin Roosevelt to sign Executive Order 8802 (Roosevelt, 1941) which barred discrimination in hiring in the defense industry. This measure was critically important because the U.S. economy was on the upswing and vigorously ramping up in America's coming involvement in World War II. Blacks, however, were excluded from the economic boom as most factories refused to hire them and they were locked out of access to the economic opportunities that were associated with the accelerating defense industry.

Randolph and others threatened to have a mass march on Washington to advocate for the inclusion of Blacks in the nation's economic opportunities. Roosevelt felt the pressure and did not want to have the mass mobilization of Blacks in a then segregated Washington D.C. that could have disrupted other policy plans that he had. Roosevelt would eventually sign the executive order despite previously saying that it couldn't be done. It was positive pressure that prevailed.

Dr. Martin Luther King Jr. and others continued to pressure President Lyndon B. Johnson in late 1964 and early 1965 for a Voting Rights Act that would remove barriers to the ballot box like literacy tests and poll taxes that prevented Blacks from voting despite Johnson having recently signed the 1964 Civil Rights Act.

Johnson initially indicated to King that the timing was not right for the Voting Rights Act because of the recent passage of the previous civil rights legislation. It was readily apparent that Johnson was seeking to spend his political capital elsewhere at the time.

The Selma campaign that began in January of 1965 by King's Southern Christian Leadership Conference (SCLC) and was supported by John Lewis and many others provided the needed pressure to eventually cause Johnson to introduce the Voting Rights Act to the U.S. House of Representatives in the days following the brutal beating of protesters that took place on "Bloody Sunday" March 7, 1965 on the Edmund Pettus Bridge. The Voting Rights Act was eventually signed later that year. Positive pressure prevailed.

It would be cynical to think that people are only compelled to move under pressure. They can also be pulled by principle, conviction, and purpose. Pressure can be used for good if properly channeled and applied. We can learn lessons from sports and efforts to change public policy on how to embrace pressure and use it for both individual and societal progress.

The Urgent Need to Challenge Devaluation

The devaluation of people based on their race has been an enduring factor that has had massive socioeconomic ramifications for centuries. The devaluation of Black people, for example, has been an organizing principle for slavery, Black codes, Jim Crow Laws, and redlining among other systems and instruments of marginalization.

Dr. Andre Perry, Senior Fellow at the Brookings Institution, pointed to devaluation in housing as a reason why a new value paradigm is needed in his book "Know Your Price: Valuing Black Lives and Property in America's Black Cities" (Perry, 2020). A study conducted by Perry et al. (2018), found that "after controlling for factors such as housing and neighborhood quality, education, and crime, we found that comparable homes in neighborhoods with similar amenities are worth 23 percent less in Black-majority neighborhoods, compared to those with very few and no Black residents. The percent difference is devaluation. In real dollars, owner-occupied homes in Black neighborhoods are undervalued by $48,000 per home on average, amounting to a whopping $156 billion in cumulative losses nationwide" (p. 15).

This is just one example of a devaluation epidemic that permeates almost every sector of American society. Devaluation has been so embedded into standard operating procedures and processes that I contend that it will take a seismic and consistent challenge to disrupt the status quo and create a new value paradigm.

Patterns of external and internal devaluation must be vigorously contested. External devaluation in this context refers to how outside entities like governments, organizations, businesses, and resource granting agencies stigmatize blackness in their assessment of who is worthy of investment, support, and equitable treatment.

External devaluation has often led to the exclusion of Black people from the distribution of significant resources. A large number Blacks were excluded from receiving social security benefits for the first twenty years of its existence because domestic workers and farm laborers were left out of the legislation. Blacks were largely excluded from those who received Federal Housing Administration (FHA) insured mortgages from the time that they were first originated in 1934 to 1968 with more than 98% of them going to Whites. More than 1600 Black majority neighborhoods were destroyed through the initiation of various highway projects, slum clearance, and urban renewal efforts between the 1940s and 1970s (Bright, 2022b). These are just a few historical examples, but the trend continues with government agencies like the United States Department of Agriculture (USDA) giving Black farmers less than one percent of grants from a program designed to help producers get through the COVID-19 pandemic even though they make up five percent of farmers (Bustillo, 2021). The economic costs of continued Black devaluation are tangible and significant.

This external devaluation too often stigmatizes blackness and leads to a subordinated status and treatment in areas such as criminal justice, education, housing, access to capital, contracting, and a myriad of other arenas. Research like that from Dr. Andre Perry that was cited above put a price on external devaluation, but the cost of internal devaluation can be just as much if not more. Internalized devaluation in this context is the persistent negative feelings and projections that individuals and communities have about themselves.

Tools are needed to combat this internal devaluation because too many people have made agreement with it and have allowed it to take residence within the minds. As the United Negro College Fund is famous for stating, "a mind is a terrible thing to waste." A mind that has internalized inadequacy and inferiority will embody what Carter G. Woodson described in his book "This Miseducation of the Negro" when he wrote that "if you make a man feel that he is inferior, you do not have to compel him to accept an inferior status, for he will seek it himself. If you make a man think that he is justly an outcast, you do not have to order him to the back door. He will go without being told; and if there is no back door, his very nature will demand one."

Now is the time for people to reimagine the possibilities for their lives and their communities and to look beyond present circumstances to see a transformative vision of what could be. This entails revisiting and retooling the value appraisal process. A more comprehensive appraisal of value can be considered and adopted.

Rather than placing total focus on disparities, people can capitalize on the assets and opportunities that they do possess. They can be motivated to repurpose themselves and investments can be made to bolster these efforts. Meaningful investment in people and communities will activate the value potential that is already in existence but may be lying dormant. It is time to take a strong and consistent stand against the devaluation of our communities and our lives.

Lessons from *Coming to America's* Akeem

The 1988 movie "Coming to America" has become a cultural classic and a staple in many American households. The movie's plot centers on the journey of Akeem (played by Eddie Murphy), a Prince from the fictional African country of Zamunda, to Queens, New York on a quest to find his bride. Though he was a Prince, Akeem intentionally made himself seem poor in an effort to find a woman that would want to be with him for his true self as opposed to his material possessions.

He identified his woman of interest, Lisa, at a community event where it was announced that she worked with her father at an establishment called McDowell's. Akeem went on to secure a position in the McDonald's-like establishment. At the restaurant, he was assigned duties that ranged from mopping floors to taking out the garbage.

A summary of the rest of the story involves Akeem eventually winning Lisa's heart, revealing his true identity, and marrying her in a royal ceremony. The story is of course more complicated (for those who haven't seen the film), but there are at least four lessons that this year's class of graduates can learn from Akeem's journey in America:

1. "One Cannot Fly into Flying"

Akeem did even the smallest tasks with a winning attitude. When collecting the trash, he once exclaimed to Lisa "when you think of garbage, think of Akeem." He took pride in doing a great job of taking out the garbage and mopping floors. Lisa recognized that and said to Akeem that she had" never seen anybody take so much pride in mopping a floor." It is difficult to compartmentalize excellence. Laziness and complacency in one area of life can easily bleed into another area. Likewise, a stellar attitude and effort on one task can catapult you into others. He put forth the effort required to be great at his assigned tasks.

His full engagement and attentiveness to his work helped him to be prepared when an armed robber (played by a Samuel L. Jackson) entered the restaurant. The challenging situation turned into an opportunity to show his bravery and force the intruder to give up his weapon. This action propelled him into an additional opportunity to work at a party hosted by Lisa's father. It was at this party that Akeem was able to make his initial inroads in his courtship with Lisa. Excelling at small tasks led him to greater opportunities. Take heed to what Akeem said when he summarized his philosophy by quoting Friedrich Nietzsche saying "he who would learn to fly must first learn to stand and walk. One cannot fly into flying."

2. Always Remember Who You Are

Akeem maintained the inner confidence of a King regardless of the position that was assigned to him. Many graduates who enter the workforce as employees will find that their workplace may be caught up in the bureaucratic dysfunction of organizations only treating their employees according to their title and position.

This may mean that your ideas and suggestions will go completely ignored because of your low position on the organizational totem pole. Don't let that discourage you from finding alternative avenues where you channel your underutilized talent and ability. This may mean utilizing your expertise to launch entrepreneurial ventures. A move like this may potentially lay the groundwork for you to escape the constraints of a conventional job and access a greater level of time and flexibility.

Akeem never forgot that he was actually a Prince and always carried himself in a dignified manner. He didn't allow himself to be defined by whatever role that was assigned to him. He was a man who picked up garbage; he wasn't a garbage man. He was able to separate his job task from his identity. Sometimes you have to do a role that you may initially think is beneath your ability to get your foot in the door in the area of your chief interest. In his case, his chief interest was Lisa.

Lisa saw his real spirit and character through his appearance as a poor man. The way that he conducted himself prompted her to choose substance over superficiality. Never let any entity or person define who you are. Always remember that the definition of who you are and where you can go is defined by you.

Akeem never let his low-level title impact his self-concept. He focused on doing his job to the best of his ability given his circumstances. There will always be those who will try to marginalize you and put you in a box. There will be people and entities who will try to put your ability in captivity. Refuse to mentally accept their marginalization. Remember the greatness that is in you.

3. Position Yourself

Akeem positioned himself for success by securing a job at McDowell's. He had to put himself in the proximity of his target in order to ultimately obtain it. Sometimes you have to go where the opportunity is and position yourself for success. The ability to be mobile is key. It is often necessary to go where the opportunity is and learn as much as you can about the environment where it operates.

This will help you to garner the knowledge and information needed to successfully navigate the path to your goal. Akeem was in a position to learn about Lisa's work and familial environment. He was in tune with her interests and was able to act accordingly to meet her desires.

Some avenues of access may be difficult to penetrate initially. There will always be those who will try to hoard opportunities. It is imperative for you to learn about the area of your desire and figure out your unique niche that will make your breakthrough possible. The chances will not be given to you. You must create them.

4. Go After What You Want

When Akeem identified Lisa as the woman that he wanted, he set his focus on pursuing her. He didn't let any obstacle deter him from his goal. Your career goal may not be a male or female companion, but you can utilize the kind of determination that Akeem displayed in your own pursuits. Many people let the daily 9 to 5 grind of a typical job cause them to give up on the dreams. They end up settling for something that they really didn't want to do.

Even when the odds of Akeem getting with Lisa seemed slim; he persisted in his efforts to win her heart. It was pivotal for him to maintain a positive attitude despite encountering adversity. Even when Akeem's father, King Jaffe Joffer (played by James Earl Jones), flew in from Zamunda to try to dissuade Akeem from his quest for Lisa, he was still able to press through towards his goal. Don't allow adversity to deter you from your pursuit of what you want in life.

Akeem was willing to go without the luxuries that he was accustomed to in order to pursue what he wanted. He knew that the uncomfortable position that he put himself in was just temporary. He understood that there is no growth in comfort and no comfort in growth. The theologian Howard Thurman once said to "never scale down your dreams to the level of that which is your immediate experience."

Get Comfortable Being Hated

I recall going on a cruise to some destinations in the Caribbean and as is customary I entered my credit card information for additional expenses that may be incurred on the voyage. There were packages on the cruise that I knowingly purchased and anticipated being charged for. Halfway through the cruise I glanced at the "account" section of the cruise line's app and noticed that there was an amount that I wasn't expecting that was being charged every day that was called "onboard gratuities".

I'm all for tipping but thought that this particular cost was already included. I didn't read the fine print but when I agreed to go on the cruise, I also authorized and accepted these "onboard gratuities".

When I thought about this scenario, I saw it as an analogy of the kind of additional costs of various kinds that people will incur on the journey to the destination of their goals. One of the major "onboard gratuities" for that people throughout history who have accomplished great things and made a significant social impact is hatred.

You are going to receive criticism and hate. You will have haters. If you want to be great, prepare to be hated. There are people who may be cheering for you to fail because they feel like if you fail then that will make them feel better about their life.

The abolitionist writer and speaker Frederick Douglass lived under the constant threat of assassination by white supremacists and attacks from fellow abolitionists that were based in merit, jealousy, hatred, or some combination of them all. The same was true for Dr. Martin Luther King Jr., Barack Obama, and others. They were all able to operate at an extremely high level in an environment of intense hatred.

The greatest sports teams are also among the most hated teams. In football, if you're worried getting hit, you're going to drop the ball. You're going to get hit regardless so you might as well score. When you get in the end zone after scoring the touchdown, it won't matter who hit you, who tried to tackle you, or who tried to bring you down.

I'm not saying to be completely oblivious to haters and their moves against you, but we must be sure to not put more focus on the tackler than the touchdown. We can't put more focus on the obstacle then we do the objective. It is one thing to be aware of something; it is another thing to focus on it. You can't afford to give your focus to your haters because where your focus goes, your energy flows. Your potential and your purpose are bigger than any hate that may come against you.

The lesson for anyone who aspires to achieve greatness in their chosen pursuit or mission is that you will not be great if you can't handle hate. Get comfortable being hated because haters and hate are "onboard gratuities" that we accept and authorize when we board the ship to the destination of greatness.

Unboxed: The Art of Fighting Off Limiting Labels

What would happen if you gave yourself a chance to live out your purpose? When we allow external labels to restrict us, or we put ourselves in a box we are taking away that chance. The feeling of being confined to a certain title, role, or position is an issue that is often and chatted about behind closed doors but rarely addressed out in the open. This is not about being unappreciative for the role that you may have for it is true that a person can flourish in a position that is assigned to them by others. It can also be true that the role that someone has for you may not be the role best suited for your bigger purpose.

I lead off with my own example of why I freely admit that I despise organizational and occupational titles being applied to me. I only list one when I absolutely must. There is something within me that resents the notion of putting my ability into the confines of a singular position.

This goes back to my basketball recruitment and experience during my high school and college career. I felt like the position that I was listed as was weaponized against me and used to limit where I could go. Because I could shoot the ball exceptional well and it was the strongest part of my game, I was listed as a "shooting guard" or a "2 guard".

The problem with that was the assumptions that came along with the position classification. It is often assumed that shooting guards don't have the ball handling ability or skillset to also play point guard. The categorization came with marginalization and limitation.

I was boxed in based on being categorized as a shooting guard. It was assumed that shooting guards who play at the higher levels of college basketball must be a certain height. This was problematic for me because I was the height of a college basketball "point guard" at 6'1 so a lot of programs automatically disqualified me based on my position classification regardless of my ability or production.

In such, my elite three-point shooting ability became both a gift and a curse. It created opportunities for me to continue my education and playing career, but the label of being a "shooter" limited where I could go and what position I played on the floor.

For the survival of my athletic scholarship, I acquiesced to the shooting guard label and suppressed my ball handling ability and point guard skills. I resigned myself to being a three-point specialist which ultimately kept me on the court and got me two athletic scholarships to two different institutions.

Looking back though, playing basketball in this limited context was not an enjoyable experience. The game became purely like a job and by the time I reached my senior season my passion for the game was almost gone.

To this day I try to use no title at all other than my name or a very vague broader one that is not easily limited. I understand that I must control the power of my own definition as much as I can because those who define you can confine you and then push you to the margins.

Labels can equal limitations if the person being labeled comes into agreement with their categorization and/or those who have decision-making authority when it comes to their upward mobility come into agreement with it.

A great example of someone who exercised his agreement

agency to fight off a limiting label was Lamar Jackson. Despite winning the Heisman Trophy at the University of Louisville, many of the professional experts, prognosticators, and other labelers said that he could never be a quarterback in the NFL. They labeled him as only being a running back or a wide receiver at the next level in large part because he was a great runner. It also may have been assumed that he didn't have the intelligence, the throwing accuracy, or the capacity to be able to read an NFL defense at a high level.

They said that he did not have what it takes to be a quarterback, much less a starter, much less the MVP. Jackson didn't let those people define him, but he made up in his own mind that he could be an elite quarterback and had confidence in his ability. He labeled himself as the MVP when others said that he wasn't even good enough to play and it manifested in real life a few years later.

He destroyed the boundaries that others tried to set for him and utilized tremendous self-confidence to break out of the parameters that were drawn for him. What Jackson used to fight off limiting labels in football, you can use to "unbox" yourself in other areas of life.

A primary strategy for fighting off limiting labels and boxes is to go above and beyond your assigned role and task. The ability to resist the temptation of hanging out on "Easy Street" and resolve to live a life on the "Extra Mile" is key. Living on the extra mile means dominating your lane and constantly finding ways to improve and add skillsets to your repertoire.

This can mean taking the time to learn other roles at your institution or organization, acquiring additional credentials, engaging in entrepreneurial pursuits, and doing your task at an extremely elite level. It is hard to box in or restrict true greatness.

To be clear, labels, positions, and roles are a necessary part of many bureaucratic structures from an efficiency and organizational standpoint. I am not advocating for people to not do the job that they were hired to do to the best of their ability. The unboxing process can entail utilizing a position to give further authorization to advance a mission that is in alignment with your larger calling or purpose.

You can operate in your gift and move forward in your mission even in the context of an assigned position. Position power, whatever it is, can be used to facilitate meaningful progress. You can define a position. A position doesn't have to define you. Take the limits off your goals. If someone limits how you think, they can limit where you go.

The Faith Factor: How You Can Use Faith to Overcome Adversity

The subject of faith is one that means different things to different people. To some it can be attached to a religion, to others it is something that is practiced but may not be formally categorized as "faith". I contend that being intentional about the proactive exploration and application of faith is a practice that institutions and instructors can emphasize to better prepare students for their careers and for life.

Faith is something within you telling you that it will happen, even if you don't know how it's going to happen. It can be stepping out on nothing and believing that you will you land on something. It is "the substance of things hoped for, the evidence of things not seen" as the book of Hebrews in the

Bible defines it. Empowering yourself as a student to deploy the power of faith can unlock the doors of your promise and potential.

Faith can not only be considered and taught from a religious perspective but also from a practical perspective. We can tap into it at any given time. It can be intentionally utilized for both individual and collective progress. John Lewis wrote in his book *Across that Bridge: A Vision of Change and the Future of America* "have you ever considered that the same power you activate in the midst of adversity can also be consciously utilized to bring forward the kind of change or transformation you would like to see in your own life? In the Civil Rights Movement, we actively and consciously utilized the power of faith to move our society forward."

He was referring to the intentional utilization of faith. Faith can be consciously employed and deployed to overcome significant obstacles. Faith is a multi-dimensional force that can be channeled and used to prepare you to face the inevitable array of adverse circumstances that are sure to come.

If there is one thing that is guaranteed across career fields and industries, it is adversity. There is virtually nothing that one can do to avoid facing adversity at some point. Adversity can come unexpectedly, or it can be something that was visible on the horizon. It can be something that people have formally prepared and trained for or it can be something that they are blindsided by. There are situations that seem to be bigger than what one has the capacity to face, when "logical" strategies won't be enough to bail a person out, but there is faith.

The more prepared you are to deal with adversity, the more you will be able to thrive in the face of adverse circumstances.

Adversity is a great faith developer. You really don't know what kind of faith you have until you are tested. Tests and trials are measuring sticks for faith. With every new chapter comes new challenges so know that you are going to be tested. You are going to have pain that you have inflicted on yourself and pain that is a part of the journey. There has never been a great lesson or a great victory without having to overcome a great challenge. The greater the faith, the greater the blessings.

A person who has great faith in the process that they are engaged in can use that faith to persevere through adversity, remain committed through trials, and pass all of the tests that are required to advance to the next level. Adversity causes you to focus on what truly matters. If you could figure it out by yourself then you wouldn't need faith. Faith is what enables you to move past your previous conceptions of limitations.

How do you tap into your faith to face and succeed against seemingly insurmountable odds? The way that you can overcome the odds and challenges is to believe and staying true to your calling. The faith-based way is to be authentic and run your own race. Everyone has been called for something unique. It is imperative to hold on to the faith that you can do it and will do it. Understand your calling and holding on to it opens the way for the persistence that is needed to achieve big goals.

It will get hard but have faith that you're on the right path. Faith allows you to overcome those turns that are a little bit harder. It doesn't allow you to get off the exit quickly. The fear will subside if you keep going. Faith doesn't retreat. You can use faith in the preparation process and move confidently through tests and trails.

It takes faith to believe that everything that you are doing is going to lead to fulfilling your mission. You have to believe it in your core and work on your mission every single day and trust and believe that things will happen for you. Faith encompasses and requires belief. It is vital for you to have enough faith to believe that you can and will become the things that they are working towards even if there is no proof that it's going to work other than you believe that it's going to work.

Faith is like working out, you have to tap into it every day. Faith requires vigilance. It is connected to patience and persistence. It is necessary to trust the faith development process. You have to build your spiritual muscles. Put your faith to work. This involves priming your mind every day. Visualization is one technique that can be utilized to strengthen the faith muscles. Visualize yourself at the finish line. See yourself there already to contend against doubt creeping in. It takes faith to believe that things will happen for you. See it and have enough faith that you will get to the finish line.

Visualization also helps to clarify goals and it presents opportunities for creativity to develop in the journey of devising ways to accomplish these aims. Creating a vision of where you would like to be and fervently believing that that vision will manifest itself is a faith workout that pays dividends, broadens horizons, and ushers in breakthroughs.

Faith can be applied to life's situations and circumstances. It can be applied to action, strategy, compassion, purpose, dedication, and processes. It can be poured into relationships, partnerships, and collaboratives. Faith is versatile and multidimensional. It can't be put into a box. Faith can be used as an instrument of deliverance. It can deliver you, your family, and your entity through adversity.

You have been using faith when you may not have even known to call it faith. You have overcome challenges because you had the belief that you could overcome them. You were able to do what you may have once thought was impossible and bigger than you though you had the capacity to get through. That is faith even if you didn't label it as faith at the time.

Faith is the transcendent force that liberates you from external and internal boundaries. Faith gives you the creativity that you need to navigate around any obstacle, to climb any mountain, and to leap over any hurdle. Utilize the "faith factor" to fulfill your purpose and step into your "Promised Land". You can do it with faith!

Humanity in Healthcare

My Mom, Vanessa Bright, used to tell me how she hated going to the Doctor's Office growing up. The reason for this was not medical; it was because it was often an all-day experience. In the Jim Crowe segregation of Alamo, Tennessee, there was no Black doctor and the "colored" waiting room in the White Doctor's office had to be completely empty before a Black patient could be seen.

The lack of humanity in the treatment of Black patients then has transitioned into other access and equity barriers that impact people of a multitude of racial and socioeconomic backgrounds. As telehealth continues to advance and the financial incentives of the healthcare industry increase; the importance of having the humane treatment of patients at the forefront is paramount. Profit is important in a capitalistic society, but it should not be placed above people when it comes to health.

When you choose to go into a profession like healthcare you are choosing to take on a high mission that goes beyond just going to work and getting a paycheck. It goes beyond transactional, but it should be a transformational calling because there is nothing more important than our health.

If you have health, you can get everything else. If you have everything else, but you don't have health, everything else won't matter. As we build career capacity it is just as important to build character capacity.

A few years ago, I was driving out of the parking garage in my building when I saw a Black man with his car hood up trying to waive someone down to help him jumpstart his dead car battery. I stopped and offered my assistance, and he was able to get his car up and running. Afterwards, he expressed his appreciation and said that he had been asking every passing car for over 30 minutes for help and no one in our building had stopped for him.

Fast forward a few years later; my parents decided to move to South Florida after retiring in Tennessee. They had just found a house to rent and were staying with me until their move in date. After coming in from dinner one night, my Mom suddenly experienced extreme back pain that prevented her from being able to sit up without pain.

She ended up needing to be transferred to the emergency room at a local hospital where she was ultimately referred to a specialist. This issue with the specialist referral was that that next availability for an appointment was in June. It was early March of that year and my Mom could not sit up without extreme pain.

She was sent back home with no clear diagnosis and not

sure what to do next as they had just moved to Florida after spending their entire lives in Tennessee. I called the man who I had stopped for a few years earlier in my building who also happened to be a medical doctor. As fate would have it, he was working for the same healthcare system that had a facility near where my Mom had moved and was able to get her an appointment with a specialist within the next few days.

My Mom was able to get seen and get an accurate diagnosis of a rare infection in her back. She would end up having an operation and being hospitalized for close to a month with a period of extensive rehabilitation to follow. Her life was likely prolonged for a few years because of the intervention of that doctor who helped her to navigate a healthcare system that initially treated her as more of a number than a human being who needed timely attention for an urgent ailment.

On January 7, 2021, my Mom suffered a stroke in the kitchen of her home while my Dad and I were there. She was taken to the hospital by the paramedics, and we weren't allowed to go as it was still during one of the heights of the COVID-19 pandemic.

With no family or friends allowed in she was completely reliant on the personnel in the hospital for anything that she needed. As she regained her bearings, we were able to communicate with her through virtual calls. She expressed confusion and tremendous frustration with regards to the way that she was being treated. So much that in my last conversation with her on the night of January 16, 2021; she told me that she wanted to write a book on "humanity in healthcare"; adding that "they ought to treat folk humanely". She passed away that next morning on January 17, 2021.

I believe that at the core of all of our research, planning, polices, and practices should be the elevation of people's humanity. The aim of seeing ourselves in others and recognizing our common need for care and compassion should be a force that undergirds our actions. The upliftment of humanity in healthcare, education, tech, and every other industry is what will guide us to brighter ways forward for a better World.

Conclusion

These essays reflect some of my thoughts on contemporary issues in America as it pertains to sports, tech, and socioeconomic mobility. There was a particular focus on populations of color that have been historically excluded from equitable access and opportunities in a multitude of ways.

That withstanding, there are opportunities to make compound advancements. Compound advancements refer to the cumulative impact of continuing to take steps forward. Some steps may be small, and some may be extremely big but all of them will add up to more people improving their quality of life and becoming upwardly mobile from a socioeconomic perspective. I truly believe that there is a brighter way forward and a future where equity, access, and opportunity will be accelerated for the masses.

Dr. Martin Luther King Jr. said that "power properly understood is the ability to achieve purpose. It is the strength required to bring about social, political, and economic change." This is a time to reimagine, reorganize, and reconstruct. This is the time to reimagine what our future can be, reinvent our possibilities, and reconstruct our communities. By drawing from the strongest of our strengths; we can uncover, study, and layout the blueprint for sustained achievement in other areas.

The brightest way forward in my opinion is for people to be more motivated to operate in their purpose in the best way that they can for their individual lives and to understand that we have the power to achieve significant collective progress in every area of our society.

References

10 startling stats about minorities in STEM. (2016, May 10). https://getcr8v.com/2016/05/10-startling-stats-about-minorities-in-stem/

Adler, P. A., & Adler, P. (1991). *Backboards & blackboards: College athletics and role engulfment.* Columbia University Press.

American Psychological Association. (n.d.). *Socioeconomic status.* Retrieved September 1, 2022, from https://www.apa.org/topics/socioeconomic-status

Asante-Muhammed, D., Collins, C., Hoxie, J., & Nieves, E. (2016, August 8). *The Ever-growing Gap: Without Change, African-American and Latino Families Won't Match White Wealth for Centuries.* Washington, DC. CFED & Institute for Policy Studies. https://ips-dc.org/report-ever-growing-gap/

Associated Press (2015, November 29). Several states trying out free community college programs. *NBC News.* https://www.nbcnews.com/feature/college-game-plan/several-states-trying-out-free-community-college-programs-n470691

Ballentine, C., & Cachero, P. (2022, June 7). *Parents are buying homes for kids priced out of the housing market.* Bloomberg. https://www.bloomberg.com/news/articles/2022-06-07/how-are-young-us-buyers-affording-homes-with-their-parents-money

Bembenutty, H., & Karabenick, S. A. (2004). Inherent association between academic delay of gratification, future time perspective, and self-regulated learning. *Educational Psychology Review, 16*(1), 35–57. https://doi.org/10.1023/B:EDPR.0000012344.34008.5c

Bendix, A. (2017, March 16). Trump's Budget Slashes Education Department Funding. *The Atlantic.* https://www.theatlantic.com/education/archive/2017/03/trumps-education-budget-revealed/519837/

Bright, M. (2017a, April 3). *Low-income students are vulnerable in a shifting college access landscape.* Diverse: Issues in Higher Education. https://www.diverseeducation.com/home/article/15100254/low-income-students-are-vulnerable-in-a-shifting-college-access-landscape

Bright, M. (2017b, April 17). *Dez Bryant And The Athletic Lottery.* Huffpost. https://www.huffpost.com/entry/dez-bryant-and-the-athletic-lottery_b_58f177e1e4b0156697224f71

Bright, M. (2017c, May 24). *Broken dreams and financial Illusions: The secret depression of black men.* Huffpost. https://www.huffpost.com/entry/broken-dreams-and-financial-illusions-the-secret-depression_b_5925e674e4b0aa7207986a5c

Bright, M. (2017d, June 6). *Uncomfort zone: Time for higher ed to address race and class.* Diverse: Issues in Higher Education. https://www.diverseeducation.com/demographics/african-american/article/15100674/uncomfort-zone-time-for-higher-ed-to-address-race-and-class

Bright, M. (2021a). *The Pickens playbook: 7 college readiness moves to make for student success.* Diverse: Issues in Higher Education. https://www.diverseeducation.com/sports/article/15108693/the-pickens-playbook-7-college-readiness-moves-to-make-for-student-success

Bright, M. (2021b, April 27). *Shaking up the athletic lottery.* Diverse: Issues in Higher Education. https://www. diverseeducation.com/sports/article/15108791/shaking-up-the-athletic-lottery

Bright, M. (2021c, August 20). *Inspiring tech dreams.* Diverse: Issues in Higher Education. https://www. diverseeducation.com/opinion/article/15114042/ inspiring-tech-dreams

Bright, M. (2021d, August 31). *Inspiring tech discipline.* Diverse: Issues in Higher Education. https://www. diverseeducation.com/opinion/article/15114349/ inspiring-tech-discipline

Bright, M. (2022a, July 1). *The Pickens playbook part 2: Year one at Tennessee State University.* Diverse: Issues in Higher Education. https://www.diverseeducation.com/opinion/ article/15293827/the-pickens-playbook-part-2-year-one-at-tennessee-state-university

Bright, M. (2022b, July 28). *The urgent need to challenge devaluation.* Diverse: Issues in Higher Education. https:// www.diverseeducation.com/opinion/article/15294884/ the-urgent-need-to-challenge-devaluation

Brooks, S. (2009). *Black men can't shoot.* University of Chicago Press.

Bustill, X. (2021, May 7). 'Rampant issues': *Black farmers are still left out at USDA.* Politico. https://www.politico.com/ news/2021/07/05/black-farmers-left-out-usda-497876

Bustillo, X. (2021). 'Rampant issues': *Black farmers are still left out at USDA.* Politico. https://www.politico.com/ news/2021/07/05/black-farmers-left-out-usda-497876

Byun, S., Ruffini, C., Mills, J. E., Douglas, A. C., Niang, M., Stepchenkova, S., Lee, S. K., Loutfi, J., Lee, J.-K., Atallah, M., & Blanton, M. (2009). Internet addiction:

Metasynthesis of 1996-2006 quantitative research. *Cyberpsychology & Behavio, 12*(2), 203–207. https://doi.org/10.1089/cpb.2008.0102

California Newsreel. (2003). *RACE - The power of an illusion: A long history of affirmative action - for whites.* https://newsreel.org/guides/race/whiteadv.htm

Center for Global Policy Solutions. (2016). *Policy agenda to close the racial wealth gap.* http://globalpolicysolutions.org/report/policy-agenda-close-racial-wealth-gap/

Chen, D. W. (2016, May 28). Dreams stall as CUNY, New York city's engine of mobility, sputters. *New York Times.* https://www.nytimes.com/2016/05/29/nyregion/dreams-stall-as-cuny-citys-engine-of-mobility-sputters.html?_r=0

Cherry, R. (2016, September 1). *The Jobless Rate for Young Black Men Is a National Disgrace.* RealClearPolicy. https://www.realclearpolicy.com/blog/2016/09/02/the_jobless_rate_for_young_black_men_is_a_national_disgrace.html

Correa, M. (2021, December 14). Tiny gain for minorities in asset management. *Miami Today.* https://www.miamitodaynews.com/2021/12/14/tiny-gain-for-minorities-in-asset-management/

Corporation for Enterprise Development. (2016). *Racial wealth divide in Miami.* https://prosperitynow.org/resources/racial-wealth-divide-miami

Dickler, J. (2021). *Virtual school resulted in 'significant' academic learning loss, study finds.* CNBC. https://www.cnbc.com/2021/03/30/learning-loss-from-virtual-school-due-to-covid-is-significant-.html

Douglas-Gabriel, D. (2015, August 17). College is not the great equalizer for black and Hispanic graduates. *The Washington Post.* https://www.washingtonpost.com/news/wonk/wp/2015/08/17/college-is-not-the-great-equalizer-for-black-and-hispanic-graduates/

Dumas, D., & Dunbar, K. N. (2016). The creative stereotype effect. *PLOS ONE, 11*(2), e0142567. https://doi. org/10.1371/journal.pone.0142567

Duncan, A. (2015, September 30). *What's ahead in education policy?* National Press Club Luncheon with Secretary Arne Duncan. https://www.press.org/sites/default/ files/20150930_duncan.pdf

Dyson, M. E., & Williams, P. (2019). *Jay-Z: Made in America.* St. Martin's Press.

Fisher, M. (2017, April 19). *How Cowboys Dez Bryant's Thoughts On 'Race In America' Got Microwaved.* CBS News DFW. https://www.cbsnews.com/dfw/news/how-cowboys-dez-bryants-thoughts-race-america/

Goldhaber, D. (2016). In schools, teacher quality matters most. *Education Next, 16*(2), 56–62. https://www. educationnext.org/in-schools-teacher-quality-matters-most-coleman/

Gordon, P., & Mora, J. (2016). *Austin becomes the first city in Texas to "Ban the Box".* Littler Mendelson P.C. https://www.littler.com/publication-press/publication/ austin-becomes-first-city-texas-%E2%80%9Cban-box%E2%80%9D

Gurney, & Kyra (2017, March 18). Lottery rakes in cash but fewer students, particularly poor ones, make cut for scholarships. *Miami Herald.* https://www.miamiherald. com/news/local/education/article139149008.html

Harkinson, J. (2015, July 2). *The combined black workforces of Google, Facebook, and Twitter could fit on a single jumbo jet.* Mother Jones. https://www.motherjones.com/ politics/2015/07/black-workers-google-facebook-twitter-silicon-valley-diversity/

Harper, S. R. (2018). *Black male student-athletes and racial inequities in NCAA Division I college sports: 2018 edition*. Los Angeles. University of Southern California, Race and Equity Center. https://abfe.issuelab.org/resources/29858/29858.pdf

Helhoski, A., Clark, C., & Beresford, C. (n.d.). *FAFSA guide: How to get free money for college*. Retrieved September 17, 2022, from https://www.nerdwallet.com/l/nerdwallet-guide-to-fafsa

Herder, L. (2021, December 27). *AP computer science principles is diversifying computer science*. Diverse: Issues in Higher Education. https://www.diverseeducation.com/stem/article/15286700/ap-computer-science-principles-is-diversifying-computer-science

Hosick, M. B. (2020a, March 30). *Division I Council extends eligibility for student-athletes impacted by COVID-19*. NCAA. https://www.ncaa.org/news/2020/3/30/division-i-council-extends-eligibility-for-student-athletes-impacted-by-covid-19.aspx

Hosick, M. B. (2020b, December 16). *DI Council grants waiver to allow transfer student-athletes to compete immediately*. NCAA. https://www.ncaa.org/news/2020/12/16/di-council-grants-waiver-to-allow-transfer-student-athletes-to-compete-immediately.aspx

Hosick, M. B. (2021, June 30). *NCAA adopts interim name, image and likeness policy*. NCAA. https://www.ncaa.org/news/2021/6/30/ncaa-adopts-interim-name-image-and-likeness-policy.aspx

Hoxby, C., & Avery, C. (2012). *The missing "One-Offs": The hidden supply of high-achieving, low income students* (Brookings Papers on Economic Activity Working Paper 18586). Cambridge, MA. National Bureau of Economic Research. https://doi.org/10.3386/w18586

Hustle. In *Dictionary.com. Retrieved September 18, 2022, from.* https://www.dictionary.com/browse/hustle

Jordan, P. [@JordanPeele]. (2017, March 17). *The Sunken Place means we're marginalized. No matter how hard we scream, the system silences us* [Tweet]. Twitter. https://twitter.com/ jordanpeele/status/842589407521595393?lang=en

Kennedy, J. F. (1962, September 12). *Address at Rice University on the nation's space effort* [Speech video recording]. https://www.jfklibrary.org/learn/about-jfk/historic-speeches/address-at-rice-university-on-the-nations-space-effort

King, M. L., Jr. (1966, March 14). MLK's forgotten call for economic justice. *The Nation.* https://www.thenation.com/ article/economy/last-steep-ascent/

Knight Foundation. (2022, June 30). *Higher education, interim release.* Knight Diversity of Asset Managers research series. https://knightfoundation.org/wp-content/ uploads/2022/06/KDAM_Higher-Education_Interim-Release.pdf

Lam, B. (2017, January 6). Obama's final 2016 jobs report marks 75 consecutive months of growth. *The Atlantic.* https://www.theatlantic.com/business/archive/2017/01/ december-jobs-report/512366/

Lien, T. (2022, September 13). *Inside San Francisco's housing crisis: 'We are not just numbers. We're persons'.* https:// www.vox.com/a/homeless-san-francisco-tech-boom

Lincoln, A. (1862, August 24). A letter from president Lincoln.; Reply to Horace Greeley. Slavery and the Union The Restoration of the Union the Paramount Object. *The New York Times.* https://www.nytimes.com/1862/08/24/ archives/a-letter-from-president-lincoln-reply-to-horace-greeley-slavery-and.html

Matos, A. (2017, March 27). Entire senior class at D.C.'s Ballou High School applies to college. *The Washington Post*. https://www.washingtonpost.com/local/education/ entire-senior-class-at-dcs-ballou-high-school-applies-to-college/2017/03/27/c15a275c-0f36-11e7-9b0d-d27c98455440_story.html?utm_term=.0fa3bb3ae0cd

Messner, M. (1989). Masculinities and athletic careers. *Gender & Society*, *3*(1), 71–88. https://doi.org/10.1177/089124389003001005

Miami Dade College. (2021, February 22). *Miami Dade College to launch rising Black Scholars Program* [Press release]. Miami. https://news.mdc.edu/press_release/ miami-dade-college-to-launch-rising-black-scholars-program/

Moore, A. (2017, April 7). *Median black family is worth $1,700 after the Obama years*. https://www.newsmax.com/ AntonioMoore/black-wealth-inequality-median-net-worth-obama/2017/04/07/id/783187/

Munoz, A. P., Kim, M., Chang, M., Jackson, R., Hamilton, D., & Darity, W. A. (2015). The color of wealth in Boston. *SSRN Electronic Journal*. Advance online publication. https://doi.org/10.2139/ssrn.2630261

National Collegiate Athletic Association. (n.d.). *Estimated probability of competing in college athletics*. Retrieved September 1, 2022, from https://www.ncaa.org/ sports/2015/3/2/estimated-probability-of-competing-in-college-athletics.aspx

National Collegiate Athletic Association. (2015, September 18). *Athletics departments that make more than they spend still a minority*. NCAA. https://www.ncaa.org/ news/2015/9/18/athletics-departments-that-make-more-than-they-spend-still-a-minority.aspx

National Collegiate Athletic Association Vs. Alston, 594 U. S.

_____ (2021) (U.S. Supreme Court June 21, 2021). https://www.supremecourt.gov/opinions/20pdf/20-512_gfbh.pdf

National Dropout Prevention Center. (n.d.). *15 effective strategies for dropout prevention*. Retrieved September 16, 2022, from http://dropoutprevention.org/wp-content/uploads/2018/03/NDPC_15_effective_strategies.pdf

National Football League. (n.d.). *The Rooney Rule*. Retrieved December 30, 2022, from https://operations.nfl.com/inside-football-ops/inclusion/the-rooney-rule/

New York City Department of Youth and Community Development. (n.d.). *School's Out New York City (SONYC)*. Retrieved September 16, 2022, from https://www1.nyc.gov/site/dycd/services/after-school/schools-out-new-york-city-sonyc.page

New York City Office of the Mayor. (2022, March 3). *Mayor de Blasio releases implementation plan for dramatic expansion of after-school programs*. https://www1.nyc.gov/office-of-the-mayor/news/073-14/mayor-de-blasio-releases-implementation-plan-dramatic-expansion-after-school-programs-to

The Next Miami. (2021, March 4). *684 high paying new jobs are coming to downtown Miami, with more on the way*. The Next Miami. https://www.miamidda.com/3-4-21-the-next-miami-684-high-paying-new-jobs-are-coming-to-downtown-miami-with-more-on-the-way/

Perry, A. M. (2020). *Know your price: Valuing black lives and property in America's black cities*. Brookings Institution Press.

Perry, A. M., Rothwell, J., & Harshbarger, D. (2018, November 27). *The devaluation of assets in Black neighborhoods: The case of residential property*. Brookings Metropolitan Policy Program. https://www.brookings.edu/research/devaluation-of-assets-in-black-neighborhoods/

Postal, L. (2016, March 9). Bright Futures budget to fall, as fewer high school graduates qualify. *Orlando Sentinel.* https://www.orlandosentinel.com/news/education/os-bright-futures-budget-scholarships-20160308-story.html

Rockeymoore, M., & Guzman, E. (2014, April 21). *The racial wealth gap: African Americans* [Fact Sheet]. Center for Global Policy Solutions. http://globalpolicysolutions.org/wp-content/uploads/2014/04/RacialWealthGap_AfricanAmericans_Final.pdf

Román-González, M., Pérez-González, J.-C., Moreno-León, J., & Robles, G. (2018). Can computational talent be detected? Predictive validity of the Computational Thinking Test. *International Journal of Child-Computer Interaction, 18,* 47–58. https://doi.org/10.1016/j.ijcci.2018.06.004

Roosevelt, F. D. (1941, June 25). Executive Order 8802: Prohibition of discrimination in the defense industry (1941), National Archives of the United States Executive Orders, 1862 - 2016. Record Group 11: General Records of the United States Government, 1778 - 2006. https://catalog.archives.gov/id/300005

Sallee, B. (2021, July 6). *SEC coach rankings 2021: Nick Saban remains king, Jimbo Fisher rises with big expectations ahead.* CBS Sports. https://www.cbssports.com/college-football/news/sec-coach-rankings-2021-nick-saban-remains-king-jimbo-fisher-rises-with-big-expectations-ahead/

Sanders, K. (2015, March 15). *Do job-seekers with 'white' names get more callbacks than 'black' names?* PolitiFact. https://www.politifact.com/factchecks/2015/mar/15/jalen-ross/black-name-resume-50-percent-less-likely-get-respo/

Shafritz, J. M., Russell, E. W., Borick, C. P., & Hyde, A. C. (2017). *Introducing public administration* (9th ed.). Routledge.

Shepherd, M. (2016, January 18). Why do many minorities avoid science? *Forbes.* https://www.forbes.com/sites/marshallshepherd/2016/01/18/why-do-many-minorities-avoid-science/?sh=29456e8d2ece

Smyth, T. (2020, March 30). What is people-pleasing? *Psychology Today.* https://www.psychologytoday.com/us/blog/living-finesse/202003/what-is-people-pleasing

Snell, K., Paletta, D., & DeBonis, M. (2017, May 23). Even some Republicans balk at Trump's plan for steep budget cuts. *The Washington Post.* https://www.washingtonpost.com/powerpost/even-some-republicans-balk-at-trumps-plan-for-steep-budget-cuts/2017/05/23/9bf202f8-3f62-11e7-adba-394ee67a7582_story.html?utm_term=.5ee6db750c98

Spears, M. J. (2016, June 1). *The distressing lack of black leadership in the NBA.* Andscape. https://andscape.com/features/the-distressing-lack-of-black-leadership-in-the-nba/

Stereotype. (n.d.). In *Merriam-Webster Dictionary. Retrieved September 9, 2022, from https://www.merriam-webster.com/dictionary/stereotype.*

Stereotype threat. (2013). In *The Glossary of Education Reforms.* https://www.edglossary.org/stereotype-threat/

Stewart, S., Chui, M., Manyika, J., Julien, J., Hunt, D. V., Sternfels, B., Woetzel, J., & Zhang, H. (2021, June 17). *The economic state of Black America: What is and what could be.* McKinsey Global Institute. https://www.mckinsey.com/featured-insights/diversity-and-inclusion/the-economic-state-of-black-america-what-is-and-what-could-be

Stewart, S., Pinder, D., & Chui, M. (2021). *Closing the Job Mobility Gap Between Black and White Americans.* Harvard Business Review. https://hbr.org/2021/07/

closing-the-job-mobility-gap-between-black-and-white-americans

Sweeney, G. (2020, September 16). *Shelby County Schools further postpones fall sports.* Germantown News & Shelby Sun Times. https://shelby-news.com/shelby-county-schools-further-postpones-fall-sports/

Tanzi, A. (2022, June 21). *US rents surge by another record, led by a 41% jump in Miami.* Bloomberg. https://www.bloomberg.com/news/articles/2022-06-21/us-rents-surge-by-another-record-led-by-a-41-jump-in-miami

Taylor, J. J. (2015, May 14). Flashback: The story behind Dez Bryant's turbulent upbringing. *The Dallas Morning News.* https://www.dallasnews.com/sports/cowboys/2015/05/13/flashback-the-story-behind-dez-bryant-s-turbulent-upbringing/

The Times Editorial Board (2017, February 4). Putting Scott Pruitt in charge of the EPA risks irreversible damage to the planet. *Los Angeles Times.* https://www.latimes.com/opinion/editorials/la-ed-trump-pruitt-epa-senate-20170204-story.html

Travis, S. (2015, December 5). Graduation rates could mean a gain or loss of big bucks for community colleges. *Sun-Sentinel.* https://www.sun-sentinel.com/local/palm-beach/fl-state-college-graduation-rates-20151204-story.html

U.S. Department of Education. (2015, July 6). *Fact sheet: Obama administration increases accountability for low-performing for-profit institutions* [Press release]. Washington, D.C. https://www.wdam.com/story/29477914/fact-sheet-obama-administration-increases-accountability-for-low-performing-for-profit-institutions/

Wamsley, L. (2021, March 18). *Before March madness, college athletes declare they are #NotNCAAProperty.*

NPR. https://www.npr.org/2021/03/18/978829815/
before-march-madness-college-athletes-declare-they-are-
notncaaproperty

Weinberg, J., & Greer, S. (2017). *Fiduciary guide to investing
with Diverse Asset Managers and Firms.* Diverse Asset
Managers Initiative. https://www.sec.gov/files/amac-
background-dami-fiduciary-guide.pdf

Wheelwright, T. (2021, July 12). *The top tech salaries in the
US in 2021.* Business.org. https://www.business.org/hr/
benefits/highest-tech-salaries/

Wiggins, G. (2012). *What works in education – Hattie's list of
the greatest effects and why it matters.* https://grantwiggins.
wordpress.com/2012/01/07/what-works-in-education-
hatties-list-of-the-greatest-effects-and-why-it-matters/

Congressional Black Caucus. (2020, July 27). *The Commission
on the Social Status of Black Men and Boys Act Passes the
House* [Press release]. Washington. https://wilson.house.
gov/media/press-releases/wilson-passes-commission-
social-status-black-men-and-boys-act

Zaw, K., Bhattacharya, J., Price, A., Hamilton, D., & Darity,
W. *Women, race & wealth* (Research Brief Series Vol. 1).
Samuel DuBois Cook Center on Social Equity and Insight
Center for Community Economic Development. https://
doi.org/10.13140/RG.2.2.10432.74249

Zernike, K. (2016, November 23). Betsy DeVos, Trump's
education pick, has steered money from public sc. https://
www.nytimes.com/2016/11/23/us/politics/betsy-devos-
trumps-education-pick-has-steered-money-from-public-
schools.html

Zhang, H. (2021, December 6). *PE firms are making diversity
efforts, but it will likely be a long road.* Institutional
Investor. https://www.institutionalinvestor.com/article/
b1vs1fdl592chk/PE-Firms-Are-Making-Diversity-Efforts-
But-It-Will-Likely-Be-a-Long-Road

ABOUT THE AUTHOR

Dr. Marcus Bright is a scholar and social impact leader who has worked across the country to build partnerships and put processes in place that have generated access, opportunities, and resources for diverse populations of people. He has published commentary in various publications over the last decade including the Huffington Post, The Grio, Miami Herald, and Diverse: Issues in Higher Education, hosted a television show that was nominated for a Regional Emmy Award, and spoken across the country on a variety of topics related to public policy, education, and social justice.

He has previously taught public administration and public policy at Florida International University, Lynn University, City University of New York Medgar Evers College, Florida Atlantic University, and the University of Massachusetts Amherst and was Executive Director of Education for a Better America (EBA); a non-profit organization that partnered with school districts, universities, churches, and community organizations in over 15 cities across the nation to conduct educational programming and enhance public policy engagement.

As the Senior Advisor for the Rising Coaches Diversity, Equity, and Inclusion (DEI) Alliance, which is made up of a dozen social justice and minority coaching organizations and is among the largest organized groups of basketball coaches in the World, he helped to lead an "Equality and Inclusion Campaign" across college basketball that included partnerships with over 150 colleges and universities.

He was a district administrator for the 5000 Role Models of Excellence Project, a school-system based dropout prevention and mentorship program that serves thousands of boys for four years as well as holding administrative posts at Florida International University, City University of New York Medgar Evers College, Miami-Dade County Economic Advocacy Trust, and the Miami-Dade County Public Schools Office of Educational Equity, Access, and Diversity.

He received a Bachelor's Degree in Government and World Affairs from the University of Tampa, a Master's Degree in Public Administration from Florida International University, and a Ph.D. in Public Administration from Florida Atlantic University.

Made in the USA
Columbia, SC
06 February 2023

11213525R00141